HLR Press
Southern California

Legal Page

DISCLAIMER: This book is independently published by, and is **not** affiliated with, sponsored by, or endorsed by any of the products mentioned in this book. All other company and product names are the trademarks of their respective owners.

This information contained in this book is for entertainment purposes only. The content represents the opinion of the author and is based on the author's personal experience and observations. The author does not assume any liability whatsoever for the use of or inability to use any or all information contained in this book, and accepts no responsibility for any loss or damages of any kind that may be incurred by the reader as a result of actions arising from the use of the information in this book. Use this information at your own risk. No part of this book may be reproduced or transmitted in any form or by any means, electronic or mechanical, including photocopying, recording, or by any information storage or retrieval system, without express written permission from the author, except in the case of brief quotations embodied in critical articles and reviews – or except by a reviewer who may quote brief passages in a review.

Respective authors hold all copyrights not held by the publisher

---

NOTE: Some of the recipes in this book include raw eggs. Raw eggs may contain bacteria. It is recommended that you purchase certified salmonella-free eggs from a reliable source and store them in the refrigerator. You should not feed raw eggs to babies or small kids. Likewise, pregnant women, elderly persons, or those with a compromised immune system should not eat raw eggs. Neither the author nor the publisher claims responsibility for adverse effects resulting from the use of the recipes and/or information found within this book.

The author reserves the right to make any changes he or she deems necessary to future versions of the publication to ensure its accuracy.

Introduction of Our Book

Hello and thanks for your purchase of this delicious panini press recipe cookbook. You will soon discover the uniqueness of this one of a kind cookbook that is packed with a variety of recipes for you to try for yourself. We made this book an easy to read and simple to understand "step-by-step" guide to making some of the best foods you could ever imagine making with this panini press grill. All right here at your fingertips.

We show you that you're not limited to just making paninis. So, we packed this guide with some restaurant inspired meals for you and your family to enjoy. Be the life of the party and use this book to make you a popular meal hosting expert!

Now dive in head first! You have about three months of meals to make here in this mouth-watering food experience manual!

Enjoy! ~ Elana, xoxo

Table of Contents

The Griddle Book of All Griddle Books

You need this book if you want to hear what we had to say about this griddle in order for you to become a gourmet chef at home. This griddler was created for those who wanted to make anything...even panini's with a grilled sandwich with other bread – baguette, Ciabatta and Michetta – besides boring white bread. You can stuff your bread with cheese, ham, mortadella, and salami to name a few ingredients. However, you can use the Panini press to do so much more.

Not only is this Griddler great for making many different types of grilled sandwiches, but it is great at making other dishes in the kitchen –fast and easy for any cook. For instance, you can cook chicken without firing up the grill, grill vegetables, make croutons, and even make dessert cakes – to name a few.

Our Reasons to Buy the Cuisinart Griddler!

Let's face it...nobody wants to return a product after you buy it/use it, and see that it does not do what you thought it would do. That's why we give you 10 reasons that we feel you should buy this product for your home!

10 REASONS TO BUY:

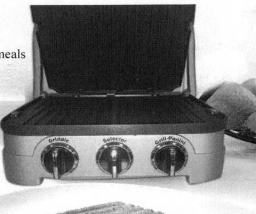

1.   Best/quickest way to make meals

2.   Non-toxic cooking

3.   High Heat Capability

4.   It's non-stick

5.   Clean up easy

6.   It's inexpensive

7.   Browns food beautifully

8.   Can act as an indoor grill

9.   Cooks multiple items at once

10. Perfect size for easy storage

Food Cooked as Good as it Gets!

Not only can you cook panini's with this appliance, but you can cook just about anything you want. Just imagine not having to pull out all of the pots and pans and just using this griddling grill accessory instead! Sounds too good to be true…right?

Panini's as Thick as You Want!

Have you ever bought a sandwich maker or Panini press in the past and discovered that you couldn't stuff it to capacity? With the Hamilton Beach Panini Press you can stuff your sandwich – or other dishes – with as much cheese, meat and veggies as you want.

The Hamilton Beach Panini Press comes stocked with handle lid lock that locks the press in place. This way you can push all of those tasty ingredients inside the sandwich – oozing with cheesy goodness.

We suggest you start stacking and stuffing today!

Cook Almost Anything with this Appliance!

···· Just a Few Simple Steps for Cooking ····
Just want to show you how easy and "FUN" cooking can be!

You guessed it, you can cook almost anything with this great appliance. We have some pics above to prove it! Get creative and never limit yourself when it come to the imagination of whipping up a good meal for you, friends or even with family.

Just remember that some foods that you may want to cook can be kind of thick and the lid for your panini press may not close correctly. If this is the case (like a thick piece of chicken above) then you can fillet cut them in half and they will cook more evenly. Just want ever you do, remember to always get a meat thermometer to check your meats to ensure it is cooking on the right temperature.

You Bet It's Non-Stick

Nothing sucks worse than making a grilled cheese only to find it stuck to the pan! Did you not put enough oil on the pan? Did you forget to grease the press? A lot of these Panini Press' comes stocked with Nonstick Surface Grids to make sure that your food cooks without sticking.

The Nonstick Surface Grids provides another healthy option for those who are health conscious. Cooking with butter and oils adds more unnecessary calories to your food. The nonstick capacity on the Hamilton Beach Panini Press ensures that you can cook without the butter, without compromising the flavor.

Features of the Panini Press

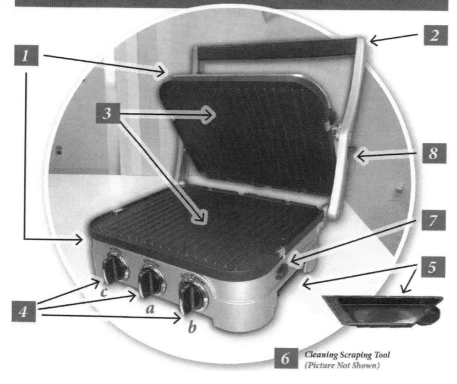

Griddler Parts & Features

6. **Cleaning Scraping Tool**
(Picture Not Shown)

Here's some features that we found on this panini press griddle:

1. Base/Cover
2. Panini-Style
3. Reversible Cooking Plates (Removable)
4. Controls Indicator lights signal Power on and Ready to Cook
   a. Selector
   b. Adjust temperature
   c. Griddle temperature
5. Drip Tray
6. Cleaning/Scraping Tool
7. Plate Release Buttons
8. Hinge Release Lever
9. BPA-Free

Put the Kids to Work in the Kitchen

You have tried different ways to get your kids excited about the kitchen. Well, let the Hamilton Beach Panini Press be another reason. It is safe and easy to use, which is a great incentive to start them off cooking with this great appliance.

From snacks, to sandwiches and even meat itself, bring the kids in for some creative fun. Have them help you start a new weekly tradition – Sandwich Sundays, where everyone can create the sandwich of their dreams and cook it right there in their very kitchen. They will be so excited about their creations that they will want to tell all their friends about it on Monday.

Experiment with the Bread...

Bread, there are so many choices to choose from that it can make your head spin. Do you remember when bread just consisted of soft, white bread that was served plain or toasted?

Sometimes it is easy to just go classic, but why not play with all of the possibilities that are now at your fingertips?

When shopping for the right type of bread you can choose from any loaf that is made with barley, buckwheat, corn, gluten, millet, oat, rice, rye, sourdough, whole-wheat, soy or even triticale. The bread aisle contains many options that can not only delight your pallet, but will pair well with the type of ingredients you are going to sandwich in-between the slices – pun intended.

Do you ever want to go for an awesome tasting Jewish, Russian or marble rye? A San Francisco Sourdough? And ancient flatbread was well known as focaccia? Or something sweet like Hawaiian?

Whatever you decide, your taste buds are going to thank you for it.
Remember, your bread choice is the most important part of the sandwich.
So, take it with caution, before you start sandwiching.

Cleaning is "Easy-Peasy"

Most Panini Press' nonstick surface makes the appliance easy to clean. No more scrubbing for hours or soaking in the sink. The no stick surface lets you clean it with cloth or Clorox wipe, toss and go. Not only is it easy to cook with, but it is also easy to clean.

This Panini Press will start to become one of the best used appliances in your kitchen. The frame of the Panini Press also lets you store it upright to save space in your cupboards for other kitchen appliances that you might need in the future.

Pro Tips from the Masters

We found that this Griddler does it all by way of cooking multiple ways all in one appliance. Cooking with this Griddler is a science. It offers five different options of cooking. Also, if you want a different cooking experience, the cooking surface for the plates are reversible plates. They also are adjustable at the hinge to be uses for contact grilling, panini press cooking, full grilling with both grill plates, full griddle cooking with both flat griddle plates. You can even mix it up to use this appliance as a half grill/half griddle. These choices are all up to you!

Remember: The different types of plates will give you different results. For example, you do not want to cook something that is more liquid on the grill plates. Some of this just makes sense..."Get it?"

10 Pro Tips from the Cooking Masters

1. **Perfect Cooked Steaks:** Never cook cold or frozen. Make sure you take your meat out of the refrigerator to get to room temperature before cooking. This will ensure that the meat is cooked more evenly throughout for a more perfect steak.

2. **Juiciest Meats:** Put your meat in a brine for a more-juicy experience: 3 cups of water ¼ sea salt and ¼ sugar. Cover the meat in a container with the brine and put in the refrigerator. Keep your brining time less than 8 hours and more than ½ hr. Approximately 1hr for every 2lbs. of meat. Pat dry before cooking.

3. **Flavoring spices:** Toss spices in a pan to extract natural flavors. You can also use a mortar to grind the spices up before cooking with your foods. This will bring out the aroma and flavors in the spices.

4. **Fluffy Dough:** When making dough from scratch take the eggs and butter out the refrigerator and let them adapt to room temperature the night before. This will do the trick!

5. **Crusting Fish with a Delicate Crust:** When cooking fish on a grill, take a brush, dip it in the mayonnaise and brush on lightly. This will ensure you get a nice flaky crust on your fish.

6. **Cook Steaks Without Oils:** Because steaks already have fats on them, when cooking, put the steak in the pan you wish to use with

the fat side down in the skillet. (even if the fat is on the side of the steak, this will ensure that the fat will cook off and be in the pan letting you cook your steaks in its own natural beef fat oil. Ymmmm!

7. ***Fluffy & Creamy Mashed Potatoes:*** After boiling your potatoes, put them in a container and let them dry first. This will make for a much creamier mashed potato! Also mash up some of the potatoes before adding mild. This will make the mild absorb better and less mess when doing this first!

8. ***Soups and Stews:*** Cook all of the vegetables in a skillet first, then add a little water to caramelize the vegetables. Make sure you let your soup cool before serving.

9. ***Pancakes:*** Always add a couple of tablespoons of sour cream! This will make for much better tasting pancakes!

10. ***Season with a Little Sugar:*** When using a little sugar, it will draw out the natural sourness flavor or tartness in most dishes, especially in a tomato based dish.

Now Get Grilling!

We found that the Hamilton Beach Panini Press is an exciting new appliance that will not only help you create new and exciting gourmet sandwiches, but it will also help you make great dishes without all of the hassle.

Placing chicken slices on the grill helps give it a great flavor, as well as provide texture from the grill marks itself.

Now that you know the press is easy to use, clean and store, why don't you take the time to look at all of these recipes and start Panini making. We promise you will not be disappointed!

Meat Selectin	Preparing	Suggested Temperatures and Grilling Times
Bacon meat	Cook with griddle plates in flat position only. We don't suggest you don't grilling in closed position.	High, until desired doneness.
Beef, boneless steak, About 1" thickness	Add desired seasoning.	Sear with the lid in the closed position anywhere between 3 to 8 minutes. You can sear the meat in the flat position, for 3 to 5 minutes per side.
Beef, filets, 1" thickness	Add desired seasoning	Sear on high heat for about 4 to 5 minutes.
Beef, hamburgers	Form burgers into even thickness.	Sear for about 4 to 6 minutes. Check for doneness. Recommended USDA cooking for ground meat to an internal temperature of 160°F (almost well done). 135° to 140°F – medium rare 145° to 150°F – medium 150° to 155°F – medium well 165° to 170°F – well done
Ham steak	If bone in then remove the bone.	Sear on high heat for about 3 to 4 minutes.
Hot dogs, sausages cooked	Cut in half, splitting your sausages or hot dogs, giving them a more grilled taste.	Cook on high with the lid closed for about 3 to 4 minutes. If using grill plates, split hot dogs or sausages. Take 6 to 8 minutes with lid closed. If grilling in the flat position, always split the hot dogs or sausages. Flip after a few minutes each side.
Uncooked Sausages	Poke the links with small knife or something to air the flavor of the links.	Cook on high and grill for 10 to 12 minutes in the closed position, depending on thickness of sausage.
Lamb (medallion), boneless, 3/4" thick	Season or marinate to taste.	Sear, 3 to 6 minutes
Pork loin chops (boneless)	Up to 1" thick. If grilling at the same time all meat should be same thickness. Watch grill time to avoid drying out the meat.	Cook on high, 5 to 7 minutes. If you are grilling in the closed position. depending on the thickness of the chops. Internal temperature of 160°F. Check with meat thermometer.

Chicken, boneless, skinless breast	Up to 1/2 to 3/4" thick. If grilling at the same time all meat should be same thickness. Watch grill time to avoid drying out the meat. If needed, pound to an even thickness	Cook on high, 7 to 9 minutes when grilling in the closed position. If grilling in the flat position, cook on high for 5 to 6 minutes per side. (internal temperature of 170°F – juices will run clear with no signs of pink).
Chicken, boneless, skinless thighs	Remove fat and pound to an even thickness to cook.	Cook on high, 7 to 9 minutes when grilling in the closed position. If grilling in the open/flat position, cook on high for 5 to 6 minutes per side. (internal temperature of 180°F – juices will run clear with no signs of pink).
Pork tenderloin	Cut into 3/4" – 1' thick and season. Can pound to an even thickness to cook.	Sear the meat, around 3-4 minutes, should look slightly pink in or meat will be dry.
Turkey cutlets, 1/2" thick	Marinade and season to taste.	High, 3 to 4 minutes.
Scallops (sea scallops)	Remove "foot muscle" (tough part) and discard. Season to taste and/or rub with extra virgin olive oil.	Sear, with the lid closed for about 2 to minutes. If grilling in the opened / flat position, sear for about 2 minutes per side. (Watch carefully for doneness)
Shrimp	Take off the shell and de-vein the shrimp and dry. Season to taste and/or rub with extra virgin olive oil.	Sear, with the lid closed for about 2 to minutes. If grilling in the opened / flat position, sear for about 1 to 1 1/2 minutes per side.
Fish (steaks) sword, tuna, salmon	Fillet's around 3/4" thick to 1" thick.	Cook on high, 6 to 7 minutes when grilling in the closed position. If using the flat position, cook on High for 7 to 8 minutes per side.
Portobello (mushrooms)	Cook 1/2" thick slices for best results.	Cook on high, 5 to 7 minutes, until nicely brown and tender.

Meals on the Griddle

Now the fun begins! These delicious and hearty meals were designed to keep you cooking very quick meals in the kitchen. We've packed a punch by adding a large variety to give you what you deserve in a recipe book like this one. From panini sandwiches, bruschetta, pizza and full cooked meals from a flat grill press to a full indoor grill, we think we've got you covered here.

See how many recipes you can come up with from the selection that we've given you to start with. This should be a fun and easy way for you to come up with some of your very own marvelous meal masterpieces! Add a little spice, substitute a different type of meat or just come up with your very own! It's completely up to you...and remember to also experiment with the different grill plates with your cooking as well. You will be surprised as to the different tastes and flavors you can make with the different surfaces this grill press has to offer.

Beef:

Lumberjack Steak and Potatoes

Steak and potatoes in only 30 minutes. This recipe is paired with frozen potatoes and frozen veggies that give you a full balanced meal in under an hour.

Position: Closed
Selector: Grill/ Panini
Plate Side: Grill or Griddle

Prep Time: 20 Minutes
Cook Time: 22 Minutes
Servings: 4

Ingredients

1 lb. Boneless beef sirloin steak, cut into 4 serving pieces
¾ tsp. Seasoned salt
½ tsp. Garlic-pepper blend
1 ½ cups frozen stir-fry vegetables

1 bag refrigerated home-style potato slices
4 oz. or 1/2 cup shredded American-cheddar cheese blend

Directions

> Preheat Cuisinart Griddler to Sear with the unit closed.
> Place the steak onto a griddle and sprinkle with the seasoned salt and garlic pepper.
> Cook on medium heat for 3 minutes on each side.
> Remove steak from griddle and add vegetables, cooking for 3 minutes.
> Pour in potatoes and cook for 10 minutes.
> When done, pour in the steak and mix together before serving.

Tender Teriyaki Braised Beef & Broccoli

Nothing is simpler than cooking everything in the same pot, and an added bonus is when it doesn't take a long time. Rice, vegetables, and beef make this entrée an entire meal in one, and the teriyaki sauce provides a flavorful theme to the dish. Just toss in, stir, and dinner will be ready in no time!

Position: Flat
Selector: Griddle
Plate Side: Griddle

Prep Time: 20 Minutes
Cook Time: 10 Minutes
Servings: 5

Ingredients
1 lb. Lean ground beef (at least 80%)
12 oz. frozen chopped broccoli (1 bag)
1/2 cup chopped green onions (1 bunch - separate white and green parts)
1/2 cup of chopped shallots
3 cups cold cooked white rice
1 cup marinade (thick teriyaki sauce)

Directions
> Preheat Cuisinart Griddler to 425 with the unit closed. Open the unit to extend flat.
> Cook beef, turning frequently, until brown adding with salt to taste...keep the juice.
> Also cook broccoli as directed above.
> Toss on green onions and shallots to griddle with beef and cook for about a minute or so.
> Add rice, teriyaki sauce. Toss as it cooks, just for a couple of minutes...till rice is cooked.
> Last mix broccoli and green onions...toss for about 30 seconds. Done!

Juicy Marinated Dijon Quarter Loin

Flank steak is a great and versatile meat to marinade, especially if the sauce is extraordinarily tasty. You can't go wrong with red wine vinegar, Dijon mustard, and lemon in anything But, imagine all mixed together with Worcestershire sauce, garlic, & black pepper! Marinade for 6 hours and get ready to wipe the water from your mouth afterwards.

Position: Closed
Selector: Grill/Panini
Plate Side: Grill or Griddle

Prep Time: 20 Minutes
Cook Time: 12 Minutes
Servings: 4

Ingredients

1/2 cup vegetable oil
1/4 cup red wine vinegar
2 tablespoons fresh lemon juice
2 tablespoons Worcestershire sauce
1 tablespoon Dijon mustard

2 cloves garlic, minced
1/2 teaspoon ground black pepper
1/2 teaspoon onion powder
1/2 teaspoon sea salt
1 1/2 pounds flank steak

Directions

> Preheat Cuisinart Griddler to Sear with the unit closed
> In a medium sized container, mix the vinegar with the oil. Add lemon juice, Worcestershire sauce, mustard, garlic, and onion powder, salt and ground black pepper. Place meat in dish and soak the steak with the marinade by pouring it all over, coating generously. Cover...put in refrigerate for 5-6 hours.
> Pour oil on the griddle. Add steaks to the griddle. (You are done with the marinade.) Cook meat on the grill. About 6 minutes per side or to your liking.

Succulent Griddle-Seared Garlic Tenderloin

There are not many basic main courses than a juicier piece of steak. The great thing about straightforward meals is that they are fast, and with the right piece of meat, they are delicious. We will keep it simple: steak, salt, and pepper. If it ain't broke, don't fix it as the saying goes!

Position: Closed
Selector: Grill/Panini
Plate Side: Grill or Griddle

Prep Time: 20 Minutes
Cook Time: 8 Minutes
Servings: 2

Ingredients

12 oz. steaks (can use 2 6oz. flat iron tenderloin)
1 tbsp. Olive oil
1/2 teaspoon garlic powder

1/2 teaspoon onion powder
1/2 teaspoon black pepper
1 pinch of salt (to taste)

Directions

> Preheat Cuisinart Griddler to Medium-High with the unit closed.
> After bringing steak to room temperature, pat the meat with a paper towel to remove moisture. Season with the salt, pepper, onion and garlic powders.
> Add oil to your griddle.
> Let the steaks cook for a few minutes turning them over and repeating after first side is cooked, then flip and cook for another 3 minutes. Turn over the steaks and cook for another 2 to 3 minutes. Check steaks to see if they are cooked to your liking, but each side should be at least brown in color.
> Slice and serve the steak after letting it cool for several minutes.

Thick Stacked Sizzling Burgers On The Griddle

Burgers: American as apple pie, which should remind you not to forget dessert. However, many people grill their burgers without realizing they can quickly be cooked on a stovetop using a griddle or skillet. With the right meat and the proper technique, the family can have burgers year-round, but try not to get addicted!

Position: Closed

Selector: Grill/Panini

Plate Side: Grill or Griddle

Prep Time: 20 Minutes

Cook Time: 8 Minutes

Servings: 6

Ingredients

1 1/2 pounds ground beef, 80% to 85% lean
9.5 oz. hamburger buns (6 buns)
1/4 stick butter (use oil as substitute if desired)
Pinch salt
Pinch fresh black pepper
6 slices cheese

Burger toppings:
2 sliced tomatoes,
1/4 onion (sliced)
2 pickles
3 tbsp. Ketchup
2 tbsp. Mustard
6 lettuce leaves

Directions

❭ Preheat Cuisinart Griddler to Sear with the unit closed.

❭ Shape ground beef into 6 big and chunky patties, then melt butter on griddle over medium heat. Lightly butter the buns, then toasting them to your desired liking. Move the buns to a clean plate. Then, using the same pan, cook the patties for several minutes. Add a pinch of salt and pepper to each and continue to cook for 3 to 4 min.

❭ Flip the burgers and repeat the process, adding a little more salt and pepper than before. Cook for another several minutes or until cooked to your desired liking.

Poultry:

Zesty Basil Crusted Chicken

This low in calories and carbohydrates chicken and vegetables dish is not only easy to cook but it is really tasty. You won't believe that it's good for you because of its amazing, mouthwatering, lip-smacking taste.

Position: Closed
Selector: Grill/Panini
Plate Side: Grill or Griddle

Prep Time: 20 Minutes
Cook Time: 15 Minutes
Servings: 3

Ingredients

Salt and pepper for taste
1 pound boneless, skinless chicken meat, cut into bite-sized pieces
1 red bell pepper, washed and diced
8 ounces mushrooms, cleaned and sliced

2 cups zucchini or other summer squash (washed, stemmed and sliced)
3 garlic cloves (minced or pressed)
8 ounces fresh basil (chopped)

Directions
> Preheat the Cuisinart Griddler to High with the unit closed.
> Season the chicken with salt and pepper for taste.
> Add the chicken to the griddle, cooking on both sides until brown.
> Pour in the rest of the ingredients and cook for 3 minutes.
> Serve

Sizzling Southwestern Cheddar Chicken–

This is a sizzling chicken recipe that has a little kick. Where is a tortilla when you need one? You can use it to sop up the leftover salsa or cool down your mouth before the next bite.

Position: Closed
Selector: Grill/Panini
Plate Side: Grill or Griddle

Prep Time: 20 Minutes
Cook Time: 20 Minutes
Servings: 4

Ingredients

1 lb. Boneless skinless chicken breasts
4oz taco seasoning
1 tsp. Cayenne pepper
Kosher salt
2 cloves minced garlic

1 chopped small red onion
2 chopped red bell peppers
15-oz. Can black beans (drained)
2 cups shredded cheddar
1/2 cup chopped fresh cilantro

Directions

> Preheat Cuisinart Griddler to High with unit closed.
> Sprinkle the chicken with the taco seasoning, cayenne pepper and salt.
> Add it to the griddle and cook for 6 minutes on each side. Take chicken out when done.
> Next, add the rest of the ingredients and cook for 7 minutes.
> Re-add chicken to the griddle and cook for 2 minutes with cheese mixture.
> Garnish and serve.

Flavored Garlic Parmesan Turkey & Broccoli Pasta

Turkey is an overlooked meat if Thanksgiving is not on one's mind, especially when a quick dinner is desired. However, it can be a perfect substitute for any of the more thought-about proteins! This particular entrée pairs the turkey with broccoli and pasta, and with a few spices it will easily convince you that chicken is not the only bird available on weeknights.

Position: Closed
Selector: Grill/Panini
Plate Side: Grill or Griddle

Prep Time: 20 Minutes
Cook Time: 12 Minutes
Servings: 4

Ingredients

¾ pound Orecchiette
2 cups broccoli florets
3 tablespoons olive oil
1 pound ground turkey
2 cloves garlic, chopped
1/4 cup chopped onion

1 teaspoon fennel seed
½ teaspoon crushed red pepper
Kosher salt
1/2 cup shredded parmesan +
more for serving

Directions

> Preheat the Cuisinart Griddler to High with unit closed.
> Cook the pasta as directed on the box instructions, and during the final minute of the pasta cooking, add the broccoli. Make sure you drain the water out of the pot.
> Return all to the pot.
> While the pasta and broccoli is cooking, add 1 tablespoon of the oil to your griddle. Place the rest of the ingredients in the griddle and cook. Make sure you cook for several minutes (6-7 minutes on each side) or until the meat is done, mixing the ingredients while cooking. Add salt as desired.
> Pour the turkey and other ingredients into the pot and mix with the pasta, the other two tablespoons of oil, and broccoli. You may sprinkle the dish with parmesan cheese before serving.

Fish:

Griddle-fried bayou garlic catfish

Catfish is a southern staple and a delightful entrée for many occasions. Despite the norm, there is no need for a deep fryer when it comes to this blackened course; the spices will exercise your senses on their own and in a healthier fashion. Quick, easy, delicious, and without the mess of batter; what else could you ask for?

Position: Flat
Selector: Griddle
Plate Side: Half Grill / Half Griddle

Prep Time: 20 Minutes
Cook Time: 10 Minutes
Servings: 6

Ingredients

1.5 tablespoons paprika
1/2 tablespoon cayenne pepper
2.5 teaspoons salt
2 teaspoons lemon pepper
1.5 teaspoons garlic powder
1 teaspoons ground pepper

1/2 teaspoon red pepper
1.5 teaspoons dried basil
1 teaspoon onion powder
1 teaspoon thyme
6 catfish fillets
1 cup unsalted butter, melted

Directions

> Preheat Cuisinart Griddler to 425 with the unit closed.
> Stir all the spices together in a mixing container.
> Melt butter. Dip the catfish to use it as a base in order to coat both sides of fish with a little bit of the spice mixture for each fillet. After seasoning, let the rest on wax paper.
> After placing fish on the griddle, divide & drizzle remaining melted butter over each filet.
> Cook the fish until desired liking or when starting to brown or flaky. About 4-5 minutes on each side. Serve hot. Mmmmmmm...delicious.

Griddle-fried garlic parmesan tuna cakes

That's right, not crab cakes, but tuna cakes! Though the Maryland delicacy is a great entrée, there can be variations within the seafood family. These tuna patties are perfect for dinner and also for lunch, and are easy enough to make at any time for you or a group. Dip in some hot sauce for extra spicy flavor!

Position: Flat
Selector: Griddle
Plate Side: Griddle

Prep Time: 20 Minutes
Cook Time: 10 Minutes
Servings: 8

Ingredients

2 eggs
2 teaspoons lemon juice
¾ cup bread crumbs (Italian seasoned)
3 (6 oz.) cans tuna, drained
¼ cup diced onion

2 cloves of garlic, minced
1 teaspoon oregano
1 teaspoon basil
1 pinch ground black pepper
3 tablespoons olive oil

Directions

> Preheat the Cuisinart Griddler to 325 with unit closed. When griddler is ready, open unit to extend flat.

> To make the paste, whisk the eggs in a small container along with the lemon juice together before stirring in the bread crumbs and parmesan cheese. Add onions and garlic, stir, and then fold in tuna until mixed is combined. Season the fish with black pepper, oregano, and basil, and then separate into about 8 full sized patties.

> Add oil to the griddle and fry each patty...each side will be about 4-5 minutes; you will know when they are done when you see them turn a light crisp brown in color.

Spiced halibut with corn succotash

Halibut with corn succotash is a refreshing summer dish and one to enjoy on a hot day, especially when you want to mix what it is in season. This dish will not disappoint. It is light...healthy and delicious!

Position: Flat
Selector: Griddle
Plate Side: Griddle

Prep Time: 20 Minutes
Cook Time: 8 Minutes
Servings: 4

Ingredients

12 oz. can whole kernel corn,
2 peppers (red and green - mix with corn)
2 tsps. Sliced green onions (2 medium)
2 tsps. Chopped fresh cilantro
½ tsp. Ground cumin

1 tsp. Lime juice
1 tsp. Honey
¼ tsp. Ground cumin
1/8 tsp. Pepper
1/8 tsp. Sea salt
4 halibut fillets

Directions

> Preheat the Cuisinart Griddler to 325 with unit closed. When griddler is ready, open unit to extend flat.
> Prepare succotash: pour all succotash ingredients into a mixing bowl.
> Cover the fish in cumin adding salt and pepper on both sides.
> In the griddle cook the fish for 4 minutes on each side till it starts browning and flakes easily.
> Garnish and serve with succotash mixture...yummy!

Mediterranean garlic jalapeno whitefish

This Mediterranean garlic jalapeno whitefish is a nice-n-light, cool and refreshing dish. One that you can complete in no time.

Position: Flat
Selector: Griddle
Plate Side: Griddle

Prep Time: 20 Minutes
Cook Time: 8 Minutes
Servings: 2

Ingredients

1 large diced tomato
1 diced small green pepper
1 diced jalapeno pepper
3 tsp. Chopped fresh basil
3 tsp. White wine or chicken broth

1 diced shallot
1 diced garlic clove
1 tbsp. Chili powder
2 whitefish fillets

Directions

> Preheat the Cuisinart Griddler to 325 with unit closed. When griddler is ready, open unit to extend flat.
> Prepare tomato mixture: combine tomatoes, peppers, basil, wine, shallot, garlic and chili powder in s mixing container.
> Season the fish with chili powder.
> On the griddle cook the fish (until brown and flakey) for 4 minutes on each side.
> Add the tomato mixture at the last 2 minutes of cooking.
> Garnish and serve.

Pork:

Spicy griddle pork & bacon fried rice

In the mood for Asian tonight, but don't want to order take out. Here is a way for you to learn how to make one of your favorite dishes, so that you can continue to make it over and over again.

Position: Closed
Selector: Grill/Panini
Plate Side: Grill or Griddle

Prep Time: 20 Minutes
Cook Time: 22 Minutes
Servings: 4

Ingredients

3/4 lb. Boneless pork loin
6oz bacon (6 slices)
1 onion diced or cut into strips
1 cup diced mushrooms
2 eggs

3 cups cold cooked rice
2 tablespoons soy sauce
1 tablespoon of crushed red peppers

Directions

> Preheat Cuisinart Griddler to High with unit closed.
> On the griddle cook the pork and stir-fry until brown, 4 ½ minutes on each side. Remove pork.
> Cook onions and mushrooms for 5 minutes.
> Add beaten eggs to the griddle and cook until they start setting. About 2 minutes.
> Lastly, add the cooked pork, cooked bacon, rice, and soy sauce, to the griddle and cook for 6 minutes or until you see the eggs start to texture.
> Garnish and add fresh ground pepper for added flavor...serve.

Sweet and savory garlic pork

This is a perfect meal to make your kids fall in love with their vegetables. The mouthwatering pork, paired with soy sauce, will provide the salted pork taste that everyone loves.

Position: Closed
Selector: Grill/Panini
Plate Side: Grill or Griddle

Prep Time: 20 Minutes
Cook Time: 12 Minutes
Servings: 4

Ingredients
1 lb. Pork tenderloin, cut into strips
16 oz. Stir fry vegetables (yellow, red and green peppers, onions)

1/4 cup sesame oil (Asian toasted dressing)
2 tbsp. Soy sauce
1/2 tsp. Garlic powder
2 cups broccoli slaw

Directions
❯ Preheat Cuisinart Griddler to Sear with unit closed.
❯ On the griddle add the stripped pork tenderloin and cook for 5 minutes till it is cooked through.
❯ Add stir-fry and cook for 5 more minutes.
❯ Pour in soy sauce, dressing, garlic powder and cook for 2 minutes.
❯ Turn off heat and pour in broccoli and serve.

Hawaiian pineapple sautéed pork

Experience the taste of the islands from your very own kitchen. Teaming pineapples, and thyme together will make you feel like you are strolling on the beach and have your taste-buds screaming for more.

Position: Flat
Selector: Griddle
Plate Side: Griddle

Prep Time: 20 Minutes
Cook Time: 11 Minutes
Servings: 4

Ingredients

1oz pineapple jam (3 tablespoons preserves)
3 tablespoons orange juice
2 teaspoons Dijon mustard
1/2 teaspoon minced fresh ginger
1/2 teaspoon curry powder
8 oz. pineapples (4 fresh or canned pineapple rings - 1/2"-thick and

cut in half, save any remaining juice)
4 5 ounce boneless pork loin chops (1/2" thick), trimmed
2 tablespoons chopped fresh thyme (see tip), divided
1/2 teaspoon salt, divided
1/4 teaspoon freshly ground pepper, divided

Directions

> Preheat Cuisinart Griddler to 425 with the unit closed. Open griddler to extend flat.
> Create sauce: preserves, orange juice, mustard, ginger and curry powder in a mixing bowl. Set aside.
> Add the pork chops onto the griddle and cover with thyme, salt and pepper.
> Cook for 3 minutes on each side.
> Pour the preserve juice and cook for 3 minutes longer.
> Transfer to a plate.
> Add the pineapple and the sauce to the griddle. Cook for 2 minutes.
> Serve on top of the pork.

Po' boy Pork Ramen

Don't know what to do with all those ramen noodles in your dorm room. This recipe pairs ramen noodles, with the flavors of pork and fresh stir-fried veggies, so well that you won't realize that you are still living on a budget.

Position: Flat
Selector: Griddle
Plate Side: Griddle

Prep Time: 20 Minutes
Cook Time: 11 Minutes
Servings: 4

Ingredients

¾ pound pork tenderloin, cut into 1/8" strips
6 ounces egg noodles
1 medium red bell pepper, cut into 3/4" pieces (1 cup)
1 cup broccoli (flowerets)

4 medium green onions, cut into 1" pieces (1/2 cup)
1 tbsp. Parsley (chopped fresh or 2 teaspoons parsley flakes, if desired)
1 tablespoon soy sauce

Directions

> Preheat Cuisinart Griddler to 425 with unit closed. Open unit to extend flat.
> Add pork to the griddle and cook for 3 minutes on each side or till cooked.
> Add broken noodles, and rest of ingredients onto the griddle
> Add only 1 packet of the roman seasoning to the griddle and cook for 5 minutes.
> Garnish and serve.

Broiled and braised tenderloin with fresh mango salsa

There's just something about pork and fruit that goes well together. The juices of both complement each other, and it's very apparent in this Caribbean-influenced entrée. Mango and lime add citrus to the spices and the tenderloin is cooked to be just as juicy as its marinade. A light and quick dinner for a breezy summer evening!

Position: Closed
Selector: Grill/Panini
Plate Side: Grill or Griddle

Prep Time: 20 Minutes
Cook Time: 14 Minutes
Servings: 4

Ingredients

1 mango, chopped
2 scallions, chopped
1 tablespoon plus 1 teaspoon oil
1 lime, zest and juice
1/2 lemon, zest and juice

1/4 teaspoon crushed red pepper
Kosher salt
1 1/4 pounds pork tenderloin 1 tenderloin)
1 teaspoon ground coriander

Directions

> Preheat the Cuisinart Griddler to Sear with the unit closed.
> Mix together 1 tablespoon of the oil, mango, scallions, lime zest and juice, lemon zest and juice, crushed red pepper, and a pinch of salt then put this mixture to the side and save for later.
> Over the meat pour a teaspoon of oil and spread around the meat. After that you will season with coriander and a couple pinches of teaspoon of salt.
> Place the pork on the griddle for 6-7 minutes on each side. Make sure you check the meat to see if it is browning before you turn it over to its other. Repeat the process.
> Give the meat about 5 minutes to cool before slicing, and serve with the salsa mixture.
> Delicious recipe that is simple and a ton of flavor.

Veggies and sides:

California meatless cilantro quesadillas

These easy to make "bursting with flavor" quesadillas take less than 20 minutes to make. This is a perfect recipe for when you want to be healthy but don't have a lot of time to make dinner.

Position: Closed
Selector: Grill/Panini
Plate Side: Grill or Griddle

Prep Time: 20 Minutes
Cook Time: 8 Minutes
Servings: 4

Ingredients

16oz black beans (can substitute with pinto beans)
½ cup shredded Monterey jack cheese
½ cup fresh salsa

4 whole-wheat tortillas (at least 8")
1 ripe diced avocado
¼ cup cilantro

Directions

> Preheat the Cuisinart Griddler to High with unit closed.
> Preparing quesadillas: cut up the cilantro very fine!
> Mix the cilantro beans, cheese and salsa in a mixing container.
> Combine mixture into a tortilla, spread evenly and fold. Continue on each until all mixture has been used.
> On the griddle add two quesadillas and cook for two minutes on both sides. (you will see the tortillas start to brown)
> Repeat.
> Garnish with avocado and salsa and serve.

Jolly green beans and shallots with sizzling bacon

Even a specific giant would appreciate this flavorful side dish, especially considering bacon is added. However, the meat is not the reason this course is so delightful; you must give the shallots and blue cheese credit as well. This could be a definite addition to the thanksgiving menu, but also accepted year-round!

Position: Closed
Selector: Grill/Panini
Plate Side: Grill or Griddle

Prep Time: 20 Minutes
Cook Time: 17 Minutes
Servings: 4

Ingredients

1 lb. Fresh green beans, trimmed
4 slices bacon
2 shallots, sliced
4 cloves minced garlic
¼ teaspoon salt

¼ teaspoon freshly ground black pepper
1/8 teaspoon ground red pepper (cayenne)
1/3 cup crumbled blue cheese

Directions

> Preheat the Cuisinart Griddler to High with unit closed.
> Bring 2 quarts of water to a boil in a saucepan. Cook the green beans for 5 minutes, covered. Fill a pot of ice water, take the beans off the heat and the immediately place them in the water. When they are finally cold then you can drain them.
> While the beans are cooking, cook the bacon, for 4 minutes on each side, until crisp. Place the bacon on something that will absorb the grease to drain then crumble the bacon after it's dry. Make sure you keep just a little bit of the bacon grease in skillet. (for flavor, of course)
> Using the bacon drippings, cook the shallots over medium heat, turning and mixing while cooking. Mix in the green beans, and season with black and red pepper and salt and cook for just a few minutes while occasionally stirring. (just enough to heat up the dish)
> Top the bean mixture with cheese and bacon crumbles before serving this delicious delight...yum! ;)

Griddle-fried okra with chicken bouillon

This side is a charming southern-style stir-fry. The beauty of the dish is that it is pan-fried instead of deep-fried, leaving it healthier without sacrificing flavor! The tomatoes and lime add freshness to the okra that bodes well with the summer air. A light and tasty side dish for any barbeque.

Position: Flat
Selector: Griddle
Plate Side: Griddle

Prep Time: 20 Minutes
Cook Time: 12 Minutes
Servings: 4

Ingredients

2 pounds fresh okra
1 medium-size red onion, thinly sliced
4 cloves minced garlic
2 large tomatoes, seeded

2 tablespoons lime juice
1 1/2 teaspoons salt
1 1/2 teaspoons pepper
1 teaspoon chicken bouillon granules

Directions

> Preheat the Cuisinart Griddler to 375 with unit closed. Open the griddler to extend flat.
> Slice lengthwise to halve the okra.
> Cook okra for 6 minutes on the griddle. Turn each of the okra frequently and cook in clusters if needed.
> In a large mixing container, combine the remaining ingredients; toss in the okra and coat. Serve.

Refreshing veggie & herb ratatouille

There is no need for the assistance of a cartoon rat to cook this easy side dish, you just need plenty of vegetables and you're set! The zucchini and eggplant give the meal plenty of substance and the spices and flavorings bring it all together. Mix everything into a sauté pan and enjoy!

Position: Flat
Selector: Griddle
Plate Side: Griddle

Prep Time: 20 Minutes
Cook Time: 10 Minutes
Servings: 4

Ingredients

1 tbsp. Olive oil
1 medium sized red onion, peeled and diced
3 cloves of garlic, chopped
1 red bell pepper, seeded and diced
1 medium Italian eggplant, diced
2 tomatoes, seeded and diced

1 zucchini, trimmed and diced
Salt and freshly ground pepper
Juice of 1/2 a lemon
2 tbsp. Fresh basil, chopped
2 tbsp. Chopped oregano
Extra-virgin olive oil to taste
Several leaves of basil, chiffonade

Directions

> Preheat the Cuisinart Griddler to 375 with unit closed. Open the griddler to extend flat.
> Add olive oil on the griddle.
> Sauté and mix onions for 2 minutes in oil, adding the garlic after and cooking for an additional minute.
> Sauté the red pepper and eggplant for 3-5 minutes, being mindful of the heat because you do not want the vegetables to burn.
> Cook the tomato and zucchini and season with salt (just for a little flavor.) Add pepper and squeeze in lemon juice. The zucchini should be ready when it's tender.
> After mixing in the oregano and basil quickly take it off of the heat.
> Garnish with basil and sprinkle a light amount of olive oil over the dish.

Sweet & simple garlic seared asparagus

There won't be an easier dish to make that provides this much flavor from basic ingredients. Asparagus goes well with most main courses, so having the vegetable as a side is always a smart decision. Garlic, asparagus, salt and pepper, and enjoy! It's that simple.

Position: Closed
Selector: Grill/Panini
Plate Side: Grill or Griddle

Prep Time: 20 Minutes
Cook Time: 10 Minutes
Servings: 4

Ingredients

1 pound fresh asparagus spears, trimmed
3 cloves garlic, minced
1/4 teaspoon ground black pepper
1 teaspoon coarse salt

1 teaspoon red pepper flakes
1 teaspoon cayenne
2 tablespoons olive oil
1/4 cup butter

Directions

> Preheat Cuisinart Griddler to Medium-High with unit closed.
> Season asparagus with red pepper and cayenne.
> Melt butter on the grilled and once melted, mix in olive oil and salt and pepper. First cook the garlic for a minute, adding the asparagus afterwards and continuing to cook for an additional 8-10 minutes, turning occasionally to verify they have cooked evenly.
> Delicious and simple...tasty meal packed with vitamins! Delicious! ;)

Sweets and desserts:

Milk dipping chocolate chip cookie

You will love this recipe. No longer will you need a mixer or a cookie sheet to make cookies. You can make them all, right here, on the Cuisinart Griddler.

Position: Flat
Selector: Griddle
Plate Side: Griddle

Prep Time: 20 Minutes
Cook Time: 10 Minutes
Servings: 4

Ingredients

3 cups all-purpose flour
1 ¼ tsp. Baking soda
1 ½ tsp. Salt
¾ cup butter, melted and cooled slightly
1 ¼ cups brown sugar

1 cup sugar
3 eggs
2 tsp. Vanilla extract
1 teaspoon cinnamon
2 ½ cups chocolate chips

Directions

> Preheat the Cuisinart Griddler to 425 with unit closed. Open the unit to extend flat.
> Prepare: combine the flour, baking soda and salt in a mixing bowl.
> In a separate mixing container, combine butter, cinnamon and brown sugar, then add the eggs and the vanilla extract.
> Add the chocolate chips and the dry ingredients and mix together.
> Divide into balls and flatten
> Place on the griddle and cook for 4-5 minutes on each side.
> Transfer onto a plate.
> Cookies will have to cool for about 15-20 min before serving...yummy!

Soft classic vanilla chocolate chip cookies

Chocolate chip cookies are the most famous cookie, and certainly one of the more well-known desserts so there have been many variations along the way. So, what's better than the best? The best of the best! Simple. Quick. Delightful.

Position: Closed   *Prep Time:* 20 Minutes
Selector: Grill/Panini   *Cook Time:* 10 Minutes
Plate Side: Grill or Griddle   *Servings:* 6

Ingredients

3/4 cup butter, softened
3/4 cup granulated sugar
3/4 cup firmly packed dark brown sugar
2 large eggs
1 3/4 teaspoons vanilla extract

2 1/4 cups plus 2 tbsp. All-purpose flour
1 teaspoon baking soda
3/4 teaspoon salt
1 1/2 (12-oz.) Packages semisweet chocolate morsels

Directions

> Pre-heat the Cuisinart Griddler to Medium-Low heat with unit closed.
> Mix butter and until it becomes creamy then beat in eggs and 1 1/2 tsp. Vanilla, until well blended.
> Steadily add to butter mixture (in a separate mixing container) the flour, baking soda, and salt, and mix together until smooth. Add the morsels and stir until they are evenly throughout.
> Spray the griddle with olive oil.
> Scoop tablespoon-sized balls onto the griddle.
> Cook for 4-5 minutes on each side. Place on a wire rack and let cool for at least 15 minutes.

Note: you can get creative with the things you can substitute (or combine) in this recipe for chocolate chips! A few of our favorites are: cranberries, nuts, raisins, blueberries, cherries, caramel chips, white chocolate chips!
If you have an idea for a substitute here...let us know about it! Give us a review and we may feature your recipe in our next book.

Breakfast:

Baby spinach and garlic scrambled eggs

This is an easy griddle dish for busy mornings. Here, you can combine baby spinach with your eggs for a healthy fast meal that will be a hit at the breakfast table.

Position: Flat
Selector: Griddle
Plate Side: Griddle

Prep Time: 20 Minutes
Cook Time: 12 Minutes
Servings: 4

Ingredients

12 oz. Baby spinach leaves
(package is fine as well)
½ cup chopped onion
1 clove of garlic (chopped)
4 tbsp. Heavy cream

8 eggs, beaten
Pinch of salt
Pinch of pepper
½ tsp. Dried thyme leaves
2 tbsp. Grated parmesan cheese

Directions

> Preheat the Cuisinart Griddler to 425 with unit closed. Open unit to extend flat.
> Prepare: in a mixing bowl beat with eggs with cream, salt, pepper and thyme.
> Add the spinach, onion and garlic to the griddle and cook for 7 minutes.
> Pour the egg mixture on the griddle and cook for 5 minutes; toss the eggs till done.
> Garnish with cheese and serve.

Homestyle bacon pepper potato breakfast filler

When you can't choose between sausage or bacon, toast or muffins. This breakfast skillet has it all.

Position: Flat
Selector: Griddle
Plate Side: Griddle

Prep Time: 20 Minutes
Cook Time: 25 Minutes
Servings: 4

Ingredients

2 lbs. Potatoes (cubed)
½ lb. Bacon

1 bell pepper (diced green)
1 teaspoon crushed red peppers

Directions -

> Preheat the Cuisinart Griddler to 325 with unit closed. Open unit to extend flat.
> In a pot bring potatoes to boil; cooking for 12 minutes.
> On the griddle cook the bacon for 5 minutes. Set aside when finished.
> Add potatoes to the griddle and stir in peppers, onion, crushed red peppers and mushrooms. Cook for 5 minutes. (making sure they start to turn a little brown)
> Stir in bacon, cover with cheese and cook eggs together till eggs are done cooking & set.
> Garnish and serve.
> Cook eggs to your preferred style. Place potatoes in a large serving dish, and top with the eggs.
> Serve while it's hot!

Spicy bacon and hash brown potatoes

This recipe adds a little heat to your palate. By combining chilies in the dish, you have decided to kick it up a notch, especially in the flavor scale.

Position: Flat
Selector: Griddle
Plate Side: Griddle

Prep Time: 20 Minutes
Cook Time: 19 Minutes
Servings: 4

Ingredients

¾ lb. Chopped bacon
3 cups hash brown potatoes
(refrigerated cooked shredded)
3 large eggs

4oz green chilies (1 can)
¾ cup shredded cheddar cheese
1 chopped medium tomato

Directions

> Preheat the Cuisinart Griddler to 325 with unit closed. Open unit to extend flat.
> Prepare eggs in a mixing bowl with chilies.
> On the griddle cook bacon for 7 minutes.
> Add potatoes and cook for 10 more minutes.
> Pour eggs over potatoes and cook for 10 minutes.
> Add cheese and tomato cook for 2 more minutes. When cheese is melted...it's done!
> Garnish and serve.

For the love of seasoned breakfast potatoes

If you love potatoes, especially for breakfast, then this is the recipe for you. This recipe was created for the spud lover and wanted to bring it to the main stage.

Position: Flat
Selector: Griddle
Plate Side: Griddle

Prep Time: 20 Minutes
Cook Time: 24 Minutes
Servings: 6

Ingredients

5 russet potatoes (peeled)
1 ½ tsp. Kosher salt
¼ tbs. Freshly ground black pepper

1 cup scallions (2 bunches diced)
1 tsp. Sea salt (coarse)

Directions

> Preheat the Cuisinart Griddler to 325 with unit closed. Open unit to extend flat.
> Season potatoes with salt and pepper.
> Place half of the potatoes on the griddle, add scallions and top with more potatoes.
> Cook for 12 minutes.
> Flip over and cook for 12 more minutes.
> Garnish with sea salt and scallions and serve.

Blissful B.L.T. biscuits

The famous b.l.t. is no longer just dedicated to lunch. Bacon is already used in breakfast, can be in every other meal truthfully, and tomatoes and kale (our lettuce substitute) are just as adaptable. Add an egg and stick in between a sliced biscuit and you have a great start to your day!

Position: Closed
Selector: Grill/Panini
Plate Side: Grill or Griddle

Prep Time: 20 Minutes
Cook Time: 25 Minutes
Servings: 8

Ingredients

1 can (16.3 oz.) Pillsbury™ grands!
™ Homestyle refrigerated
buttermilk biscuits
8 slices thick-cut maple bacon
1/4 cup packed brown sugar

8 pasteurized eggs*
1 handful fresh kale leaves
1 large avocado, pitted, peeled
and sliced
1 large tomato, cut into 8 slices

Directions

> Preheat the Cuisinart Griddler to Medium-Heat with unit closed.
> Place the can of refrigerated buttermilk biscuits, the sides are allowed to touch so don't worry about them touching. Cook for 4-5 minutes on each side
> Place the bacon on the griddle and cook for 8 minutes on each side. Use a silicone spatula to scrape excess grease that runs along the sides of the bacon.
> Next, it's time to bring the sandwiches together. Slice open each biscuit, splitting evenly across the middle.
> You may cook the eggs to your liking.
> Work in layers from the bottom biscuit up: kale leaves, avocado, tomato, egg, then bacon. Put the top biscuit on and you're sandwich.
> This is what you call "breakfast, lunch or dinner!" Yummm... ;)

Sweet and soft French toast fingers

Cinnamon, vanilla, maple syrup, and yogurt; there's not much else to say except for the fact that these French toast sticks will be a hit with the entire family. There is a double dose of ingredients with the toast and the sauce so there will be plenty of flavor to go around!

Position: Flat
Selector: Griddle
Plate Side: Griddle

Prep Time: 20 Minutes
Cook Time: 4 Minutes
Servings: 2

Ingredients

4 eggs
½ cup vanilla nonfat Greek yogurt
1/4 tsp. Powdered sugar
¼ tsp. Ground cinnamon
4 slices wide-loaf day-old bread

Sauce
¾ cup vanilla nonfat Greek yogurt
¼ cup pancake syrup
1/8 tsp. Ground cinnamon

Directions

> Preheat the Cuisinart Griddler to 325 with unit closed. Open unit to extend flat.
> Create sauce by combining Greek yogurt, pancake syrup, and cinnamon.
> Using a separate dish, beat eggs and blend in yogurt, powdered sugar, and cinnamon.
> Slice each piece of bread into 4 sticks. Immerse each side of each stick in the egg mixture.
> Cook each bread stick, in batches if necessary, for 1-2 minutes on each side, reducing the heat slightly if needed. There should be no liquid remains visible. If needed, clean the griddle between batches.

Fresh omelets, oh my!

Omelets are a breakfast and brunch basic, and they are incredibly easy to make! Besides being simple and classic, the breakfast dish is also very versatile and a variety of ingredients can be used to cook up what you crave the most. Onions, peppers, mushrooms, cheese, scallions, pepperoni, whatever you want, you can't go wrong.

Position: Flat
Selector: Griddle
Plate Side: Griddle

Prep Time: 20 Minutes
Cook Time: 5 Minutes
Servings: 1

Ingredients

2-3 eggs
Salt and pepper, to taste
2 cloves minced garlic

1/4 cup chopped onion
2-3 tsp. Butter (can use less with nonstick pan)

Directions

> Preheat the Cuisinart Griddler to 325 with unit closed. Open unit to extend flat.
> Beat the 2-3 eggs and season as desired.
> Add butter to the griddle. Then add the egg mixture. Allow the eggs to set up for 30 sec; sliding the pan back & forth very gently. Let it set for just another min.
> Lift the edge of the egg mixture carefully with spatula allowing the liquid on top to touch the surface of the griddle. (You can also use a fork or something flat to achieve this result) repeat this step around the entire omelet making sure the eggs are set up evenly around the omelet. If the omelet is moving around easily, but staying together, it's ready.

The essential toasted breakfast sandwich

Simple is probably the most underrated characteristic in recipes. Sometimes we just need to get back to basics because the best lies within. Bacon, eggs, cheese, and toast all in one! Fruit makes the perfect garnish, and everything you need is right in front of you (coffee optional, if needed).

Position: Flat
Selector: Griddle
Plate Side: Griddle

Prep Time: 20 Minutes
Cook Time: 8 Minutes
Servings: 2

Ingredients

2 eggs
2 tbsp. Milk or water
3 tsp. Butter, room temperature, divided

4 slices bread of choice
2 slices cheese of choice
4 slices fully-cooked bacon
1/4 tsp. Basil

Directions

> Preheat the Cuisinart Griddler to 325 with unit closed. Open unit to extend flat.
> Whisk together eggs, milk, salt and pepper.
> Melt 1 teaspoon butter on the griddle. Add the egg mixture, and carefully mix back and forth with a spatula just for a minute, just until they start to set up. Cook until thick and there is no visible liquid to the eggs & there is no stirring necessary. Clean the griddle before the next step.
> Butter one side of each slice of bread. Grill the bread, buttered side against the surface of the griddle, and top each with scrambled eggs, cheese and bacon. Put the other slices of on top of the ingredients, with the buttered side up this time.
> Cook 2-4 minutes, flipping the sandwich halfway through.
> Makes a yummy treat for breakfast, lunch or dinner... ;)

Keepin' It "Crispy!"

Honey Dijon pigs in a blanket with tangy mustard sauce

These are an easy appetizer to make or the perfect finger food when you're using the BBQ. They've got a delicious depth of flavor thanks the mustard.

Position: Closed
Selector: Grill/Panini
Plate Side: Grill or Griddle

Prep Time: 20 Minutes
Cook Time: 15 Minutes
Servings: 4-6

Ingredients:

1 8-ounce can of Crescent rolls
Mustard sauce:
¼ cup Dijon mustard
½ cup sour cream
20 mini hot dogs or cocktail franks

½ cup mayonnaise
1 egg, lightly beaten
3 tablespoons Dijon mustard
1 tablespoon whole-grain Mustard

Directions

> Preheat the Cuisinart Griddler to Medium with unit closed.
> Slice each piece of dough into 3 equal pieces lengthwise.
> Lightly coat the dough with the Dijon with a brush, and place a hot dog in each piece of dough. Make sure the hot dogs are put on one side of the dough and roll the dough around the hot dogs.
> Place the rolled up hot dogs in the griddle. Make sure the seam side is down, and brush with the beaten egg. Add poppy seeds or sesame seeds to the top if desired.
> Cook for around 12-15 minutes. They will be golden brown when ready.
> While the pigs in a blanket are cooking, mix all the dip ingredients in a bowl. Refrigerate the dip until it's time to serve the pigs in a blanket.
> Serve the pigs in a blanket hot.

Garlic flavored bacon cheesy fries

There's nothing better than French fries, except when you add bacon and cheese. The best part is there's no oil used so they're healthier

Position: Closed
Selector: Grill/Panini
Plate Side: Grill or Griddle

Prep Time: 20 Minutes
Cook Time: 22 Minutes
Servings: 3

Ingredients
3 strips cooked bacon
½ cup shredded cheese

1 package frozen fries
1 tbsp. Garlic powder

Directions
> Preheat the Cuisinart Griddler to Medium heat with unit closed.
> Put the fries in a single layer on the griddle and cook for 15-20 minutes. They will be golden brown when finished
> Preheat your broiler
> Sprinkle the cheese on the fries and top with bacon. Sprinkle the garlic powder over the top of the cheese. Broil for 1-2 minutes until the cheese melts.
> Serve immediately.

Baked lemon thyme chicken wings

These wings have a great citrus flavor that mixes well with the woodsy flavor of the thyme. The best part is there's very little prep time.

Position: Flat
Selector: Griddle
Plate Side: Half Grill/ Half Griddle

Prep Time: 20 Minutes
Cook Time: 15-20 Minutes
Servings: 8

Ingredients:

4 pounds chicken wings, cut in half at joint (wing tips removed)
1/4 cup fresh lemon juice
1 tablespoon ground pepper
1 tablespoon garlic powder
1 tablespoon onion powder
2 teaspoons coarse salt

2 teaspoons dried thyme crushed
1/2 teaspoon cayenne pepper
1/4 cup (1/2 stick) unsalted butter, melted
Blue cheese or ranch dressing, or barbecue sauce, for dipping

Directions

> Insert one plate on its grill side and another on its griddle side. Preheat the Cuisinart Griddler to 425 with the unit closed. Open unit to extend flat.

> Toss the lemon juice and chicken in a big bowl. Then mix in the pepper, thyme, salt and pepper, garlic powder, and onion powder. Then mix in the bitter and cayenne.

> Place the chicken wings on your griddle in a single layer. Cook the chicken for 15-20 minutes, turning ½ way and checking occasionally for doneness.

> Serve immediately with sauce of your choice.

Baked adobo lime steak fajitas

Adobo is a Puerto Rican seasoning mix that is packed with exotic flavor. It pairs well with the citrus flavor with the lime.

Position: Flat
Selector: Griddle
Plate Side: Half Grill /Half Griddle

Prep Time: 20 Minutes
Cook Time: 20 Minutes
Servings: 3-4

Ingredients:

1 lb. Thin sirloin steak, slice in
1/4" strips
1 white onion sliced
1 red bell pepper, sliced
1 green bell pepper, sliced

1 tbsp. oil
3 tsp adobo
Juice from 2 limes
Flour or white corn tortillas

Directions

> Insert one plate on its grill side and another on its griddle side. Preheat the Cuisinart Griddler to 425 with the unit closed. Open unit to extend flat.
> Place the oil, adobo, and lime juice in a bowl and mix well. Then toss the steak and vegetable in the mixture
> Place the ingredient on your griddle. Cook for 20 minutes
> Serve immediately with tortillas

Cajun "square griddle fried" fish strips

This is a kicked-up version of the fish from fish and chips. The Cajun seasoning and the garlic add a world of flavor. Yum!

Position: Flat
Selector: Griddle
Plate Side: Half Grill /Half Griddle

Prep Time: 20 Minutes
Cook Time: 15 Minutes
Servings: 4

Ingredients:

1 1/2 pounds skinless, boneless Pollock (or other firm white fish), cut into 2-by-4" pieces
2 3/4 cups crispy rice cereal, crushed

3 teaspoons Cajun seasoning
2 garlic clove finely minced
Kosher salt
Black pepper
3 large eggs

Directions

> Insert one plate on its grill side and another on its griddle side. Preheat the Cuisinart Griddler to 425 with the unit closed. Open unit to extend flat.

> Mix together the cereal, garlic, seasoning, and pepper in a bowl.

> Whisk the eggs with a pinch of salt, until the mixture becomes frothy.

> Dip the fish in the egg mixture and then the cereal mixture.

> Place the fish on the griddle and cook until the fish is cooked through, around 15 minutes.

> Serve immediately, with fries if desired.

Beef Panini's Galore

Cabbage and Corned Beef Panini

This is a perfect way to combine these two favorites. The Muenster makes for a tasty texture contrast to the corned beef and cabbage.

Position: Closed
Selector: Grill/Panini
Plate Side: Grill or Griddle

Prep Time: 20 Minutes
Cook Time: 4 Minutes
Servings: 2

Ingredients:

1 cup thinly sliced green cabbage
1 tbsps. olive oil
¼ tsp. table salt
Freshly ground black pepper
1 tsp. yellow mustard seeds
2 tbsps. unsalted butter, softened
4 1/2"-thick slices rye bread with caraway seeds

1 tbsps. grainy mustard, more to taste
12 thin slices (6 oz.) corned beef
6 thin slices (3 oz.) Muenster cheese
¼ cup water

Directions:

> Preheat Cuisinart Griddler to Medium-High with the lid closed.
> Mix the water, cabbage, olive oil, mustard seeds, salt, and pepper in a saucepan, heat on medium-high heat until water boils. Once boiling lower heat to medium-low heat, cover, allow the mixture to cook for 10 to 15 minutes, stirring every once in a while. Remove the cabbage from the saucepan, and set aside any remaining water in the pan.
> Butter one side of each piece of bread and place mustard on the other side. Top two pieces of bread, mustard side up with corned beef, then cabbage, and finally cheese. Top with the remaining pieces of bread, butter side up.
> Cook the sandwiches for 4 to 6 minutes on medium heat, and make sure to check halfway through. The bread should be brown, and the cheese should be melted.

Mozzarella and Pesto Beef Panini

This is filled will lots of classic Italian flavor. The pesto provides an aromatic flavor that pairs well with the creaminess of the mozzarella, and the rich flavor of beef.

Position: Closed
Selector: Grill/Panini
Plate Side: Grill or Griddle

Prep Time: 15 Minutes
Cook Time: 4 Minutes
Servings: 4

Ingredients:

8 slices Italian bread, 1/2" thick
2 tbsps. butter or margarine, softened
1/2 cup basil pesto
1/2 lb. thinly sliced cooked deli roast beef

4 slices (1 oz. each) mozzarella cheese
Marinara sauce, warmed, if desired

Directions:

> Preheat the Cuisinart Griddler to Medium-High with unit closed.
> Spread the pesto on one side of each piece of bread. Spread the butter on the other side.
> Split the roast beef between four pieces of bread with the pesto side up and then top with the mozzarella. Place the other piece of bread on the mozzarella with the butter side up.
> Cook the Panini on medium heat for 3-4 minutes, checking halfway through. The bread should be brown, and the cheese should be melted

Classic Patty Melt Panini

This is a classic diner favorite. The rye bread, and onions give this sandwich loads of flavor.

Position: Closed
Selector: Grill/Panini
Plate Side: Grill or Griddle

Prep Time: 15 Minutes
Cook Time: 4 Minutes
Servings: 4

Ingredients:

2 tbsps. unsalted butter
1 large Vidalia or other sweet
onion, sliced
1 lb. lean ground beef
1 tbsp. Worcestershire sauce
1/2 tsp garlic powder

1/2 tsp dried oregano
1/4 tsp black pepper
8 slices seedless rye
1/4 lb. thinly sliced reduced-fat
American cheese, about 8 slices
1/4 cup light Thousand Island
salad dressing

Directions:

> Preheat the Cuisinart Griddler to Sear with unit closed.
> Melt the butter on the griddle. Add the onions and cook for about 20 minutes. While the onions are cooking combine the beef, Worcestershire sauce, and the seasoning. Form the beef into patties that are similar in shape to the bread. Place the patties on the griddle with the onions for the last 5 minutes of cooking. Flip the meat once halfway through
> Put a slice of cheese on a piece of bread then a patty, the onions and top with another slice of cheese and top with another piece of bread. Repeat the process with the remaining sandwiches.
> Cook the sandwiches for 4 minutes, and make sure to check halfway through. The bread should be brown, and the cheese should be melted. Serve the sandwiches with a side of the Thousand Island dressing.

Buffalo Melt Patty Panini

These are perfect for game day. The give this sandwich a lovely kick that's balanced perfectly by the cheese

Position: Closed
Selector: Grill/Panini
Plate Side: Grill or Griddle

Prep Time: 15 Minutes
Cook Time: 4 Minutes
Servings: 4

Ingredients:

2 tbsps. unsalted butter
1 large Vidalia or other sweet onion, sliced
1 lb. lean ground beef
1 tbsp. Worcestershire sauce
1/2 tsp garlic powder
1/4 tsp black pepper

8 slices seedless rye
1/4 lb. thinly sliced Swiss cheese, about 8 slices
1/4 cup blue cheese dressing
1 cup mayonnaise
1 cup buffalo hot sauce

Directions:

> Preheat the Cuisinart Griddler to Sear with unit closed.
> Melt the butter on the griddle. Add the onions and cook for about 20 minutes. While the onions are cooking combine the beef, Worcestershire sauce, and the seasoning. Form the beef into patties that are similar in shape to the bread. Place the patties in the griddle with the onions for the last 5 minutes of cooking. Flip the meat once halfway through.
> Mix the buffalo sauce and mayonnaise in a medium bowl.
> Spread the buffalo sauce mixture on one side of each piece of bread.
> Put a slice of cheese on a piece of bread then a patty, the onions and top with another slice of cheese and top with another piece of bread. Repeat the process with the remaining sandwiches.
> Cook the sandwiches for 4 minutes on medium heat, and make sure to check halfway through. The bread should be brown, and the cheese should be melted. Serve the sandwiches with a side of the blue cheese dressing.

Babba Ghanoush and Feta Lamb Panini

This is a great way to use leftover lamb. The beautiful Mediterranean flavors hit the spot, and the grilled pita or flatbread is delicious.

Position: Closed
Selector: Grill/Panini
Plate Side: Grill or Griddle

Prep Time: 20 Minutes
Cook Time: 3-4 Minutes
Servings: 4

Ingredients:

1 cup grilled eggplant pulp (can)
1 small clove garlic, coarsely chopped
1 tbsp. tahini (sesame paste)
1/2 medium lemon
Salt to taste
Freshly ground black pepper

2 to 3 sprigs flat-leaf parsley, chopped
8 to 12 ounces roasted leg of lamb
4 oval pita breads or flatbreads, cut in half horizontally
1 to 2 tbsps. olive oil
3/4 cup crumbled feta cheese

Directions:

> Preheat the Cuisinart Griddler to Medium-High with unit closed.
> Place the eggplant, garlic, 1 tsp lemon juice, and tahini in a food processor. Pulse the mixture until it becomes smooth, and then salt and pepper to taste.
> Slice the lamb into bite sized piece. If you use pita bread use a brush to lightly coat both sides with olive oil. If you're using flatbread just coat one side.
> Spread the Babba Ghanoush spread on one side of the bread. If you're using flatbread make sure it's not the side with olive oil. Put the lamb on top of the Babba Ghanoush, then top with the feta, and finally sprinkle with the parsley. Top with another piece of pita or flatbread. Make sure the oil side is up if you're using flatbread
> Cook the sandwiches for 4 minutes, and make sure to check halfway through.

Lamb and Havarti Grilled Cheese Panini

Your lamb leftovers are calling for this easy sandwich. The Havarti adds delicious creamy balance to the lamb and the spinach gives it a nice crunch.

Position: Closed
Selector: Grill/Panini
Plate Side: Grill or Griddle

Prep Time: 10 Minutes
Cook Time: 4 Minutes
Servings: 2

Ingredients:

4 slices thick hearty bread
2 tbsp. butter, room temperature
1 cup Havarti, shredded
1/2 cup leftover lamb, reheated

sliced red onion
handful of spinach
4 tbsps. tzatziki, room
temperature

Directions:

> Preheat the Cuisinart Griddler to Medium-High with unit closed.
> Spread butter on one side of each piece of bread.
> Place a layer of cheese down, then the lamb, spinach onions, and tzatziki on one piece of bread. Make sure it's not on the buttered side. Then top with the other piece of bread, making sure the buttered side is up.
> Cook the sandwiches 4 minutes, and make sure to flip halfway through. The bread should be brown, and the cheese should be melted.

Spicy Beefy & Horseradish Cheese Panini

This will hit the spot for any meat lover. The horseradish and jalapeno give this sandwich some nice heat that's balanced perfectly by the cheese

Position: Closed
Selector: Grill/Panini
Plate Side: Grill or Griddle

Prep Time: 20 Minutes
Cook Time: 4 Minutes
Servings: 4

Ingredients:

1/3 cup mayonnaise
1/4 cup crumbled blue cheese
2 tsps. prepared horseradish
1/8 tsp pepper
1 large sweet onion, thinly sliced
1 tbsp. olive oil

8 slices white bread
8 slices provolone cheese
8 slices deli roast beef
2 tbsps. butter, softened
12 small jalapeno slices

Directions:

> Preheat the Cuisinart Griddler to High with unit closed.
> Combine the mayonnaise, blue cheese, horseradish and pepper in a nice size bowl.
> Sauté the onions in a skillet on medium heat until they become nice and tender.
> Spread the bleu cheese mixture onto a single side of each piece of the bread.
> Place a layer of cheese, then jalapenos, beef, onions and then a second layer of cheese on half the pieces of bread. Place the other slices of bread on top.
> Butter the top and bottom of the sandwich and cook the Panini for 6 minutes, flipping halfway through. The bread should be brown, and the cheese should be melted.

Mozzarella and Pesto Beef Panini

This is filled will lots of classic Italian flavor. The pesto provides an aromatic flavor that pairs well with the creaminess of the mozzarella, and the rich flavor of beef.

Position: Closed
Selector: Grill/Panini
Plate Side: Grill or Griddle

Prep Time: 15 Minutes
Cook Time: 4Minutes
Servings: 4

Ingredients:

8 slices Italian bread, 1/2" thick
2 tbsps. butter or margarine,
softened
1/2 cup basil pesto
1/2 lb. thinly sliced cooked deli
roast beef

4 slices (1 oz. each) mozzarella
cheese
Marinara sauce, warmed, if
desired

Directions:

❯ Preheat the Cuisinart Griddler to High with unit closed.
❯ Spread the pesto on one side of each piece of bread. Spread the butter on the other side.
❯ Split the roast beef between four pieces of bread with the pesto side up and then top with the mozzarella. Place the other piece of bread on the mozzarella with the butter side up.
❯ Cook the Panini for 4 minutes, checking halfway through. The bread should be brown, and the cheese should be melted

Healthier Turkey Patty Melt Panini

This is a classic diner favorite. The rye bread, and onions give this sandwich loads of flavor.

Position: Closed
Selector: Grill/Panini
Plate Side: Grill or Griddle

Prep Time: 25 Minutes
Cook Time: 4 Minutes
Servings: 4

Ingredients:

2 tbsps. unsalted butter
1 large Vidalia or other sweet
onion, sliced
1 lb. lean ground turkey
1 tbsp. Worcestershire sauce
1/2 tsp garlic powder

1/2 tsp dried oregano
1/4 tsp black pepper
8 slices seedless rye
1/4 lb. thinly sliced reduced-fat
American cheese, about 8 slices
1/4 cup light Thousand Island
salad dressing

Directions:

> Melt the butter in a large skillet on medium heat. Add the onions and cook for about 20 minutes. While the onions are cooking combine the ground turkey, Worcestershire sauce, and the seasoning. Form the beef into patties that are similar in shape to the bread. Place the patties in the skillet with the onions for the last 5 minutes of cooking. Flip the meat once halfway through

> Put a slice of cheese on a piece of bread then a patty, the onions and top with another slice of cheese and top with another piece of bread. Repeat the process with the remaining sandwiches.

> Preheat the Cuisinart Griddler to Medium-High with the unit closed.

> Cook the sandwiches for 4 minutes on medium heat, and make sure to check halfway through. The bread should be brown, and the cheese should be melted. Serve the sandwiches with a side of the Thousand Island dressing.

Buffalo Tuna Melt Panini

These are perfect for game day. The give this sandwich a lovely kick that's balanced perfectly by the cheese

Position: Closed
Selector: Grill/Panini
Plate Side: Grill or Griddle

Prep Time: 25 Minutes
Cook Time: 4 Minutes
Servings: 4

Ingredients:

2 tbsps. unsalted butter
1 large Vidalia or other sweet onion, sliced
1 lb. tuna in a can
1 tbsp. Worcestershire sauce
1/2 tsp garlic powder
1/4 tsp black pepper

8 slices seedless rye
1/4 lb. thinly sliced Swiss cheese, about 8 slices
1/4 cup blue cheese dressing
1 cup mayonnaise
1 cup buffalo hot sauce

Directions:

> Melt the butter in a large skillet on medium heat. Add the onions and cook for about 20 minutes. While the onions are cooking combine the beef, Worcestershire sauce, and the seasoning. Form the tuna into patties that are similar in shape to the bread. Place the patties in the skillet with the onions for the last 5 minutes of cooking. Flip the meat once halfway through.
> Mix the buffalo sauce and mayonnaise in a medium bowl.
> Spread the buffalo sauce mixture on one side of each piece of bread.
> Put a slice of cheese on a piece of bread then a patty, the onions and top with another slice of cheese and top with another piece of bread. Repeat the process with the remaining sandwiches.
> Preheat the Cuisinart Griddler to Medium-High with the unit closed.
> Cook the sandwiches for 4 minutes on medium heat, and make sure to check halfway through. The bread should be brown, and the cheese should be melted. Serve the sandwiches with a side of the blue cheese dressing.

Turkish Style Feta and Roast Beef Panini

This is a great way to use leftover roast beef. The beautiful Mediterranean flavors hit the spot, and the grilled pita or flatbread is delicious.

Position: Closed
Selector: Grill/Panini
Plate Side: Grill or Griddle

Prep Time: 20 Minutes
Cook Time: 4 Minutes
Servings: 4

Ingredients:

1 cup grilled eggplant pulp (can)
1 small clove garlic, coarsely chopped
1 tbsp. tahini (sesame paste)
1/2 medium lemon
Salt
Freshly ground black pepper

2 to 3 sprigs flat-leaf parsley, chopped
8 to 12 ounces roast beef
4 oval pita breads or flatbreads, cut in half horizontally
1 to 2 tbsps. olive oil
3/4 cup crumbled feta cheese

Directions:

> Preheat the Cuisinart Griddler to Medium-High with the unit closed.
> Place the eggplant, garlic, 1 tsp lemon juice, and tahini in a food processor. Pulse the mixture until it becomes smooth, and then salt and pepper to taste.
> Slice the roast beef into bite sized piece. If you use pita bread use a brush to lightly coat both sides with olive oil. If you're using flatbread just coat one side.
> Spread the mixture on one side of the bread. If you're using flatbread make sure it's not the side with olive oil. Put the roast beef on top of the mixture, then top with the feta, and finally sprinkle with the parsley. Top with another piece of pita or flatbread. Make sure the oil side is up if you're using flatbread
> Cook the sandwiches for 4 to 5 minutes, and make sure to check halfway through.

Roast Beef and Havarti Grilled Cheese Panini - repeat

Your roast beef leftovers are calling for this easy sandwich. The Havarti adds delicious creamy balance to the lamb and the spinach gives it a nice crunch.

Position: Closed
Selector: Grill/Panini
Plate Side: Grill or Griddle

Prep Time: 10 Minutes
Cook Time: 4 Minutes
Servings: 1

Ingredients:

2 slices thick hearty bread
1 tbsp. butter, room temperature
1/2 cup Havarti, shredded
1/4 cup leftover roast beef, reheated

sliced red onion
handful of spinach
2 tbsps. tzatziki, room temperature

Directions:

> Preheat the Cuisinart Griddler to Medium-High with the unit closed.
> Spread butter on one side of each piece of bread.
> Place a layer of cheese down, then the lamb, spinach onions, and tzatziki on one piece of bread. Make sure it's not on the buttered side. Then top with the other piece of bread, making sure the buttered side is up.
> Cook the sandwiches 4 minutes, and make sure to check halfway through. The bread should be brown, and the cheese should be melted.

Roasted Garlic Mayonnaise and Lamb Panini with Thyme

The beautiful flavor of the lamb is highlighted in this sandwich. The roasted garlic adds a sweet flavor that pairs well with the thyme and mayonnaise.

Position: Closed
Selector: Grill/Panini
Plate Side: Grill or Griddle

Prep Time: 10 Minutes
Cook Time: 5 Minutes
Servings: 4

Ingredients:

12 thin slices boneless, roasted leg of lamb
2 heads garlic
1/2 cup mayonnaise
2 tbsps. lemon juice
1 tbsp. fresh thyme leaves

Salt and freshly ground black pepper
4 paper-thin slices sweet onion
Fresh spinach leaves
1 large tomato, thinly sliced
4 soft sandwich rolls
Olive oil

Directions:

> Preheat your oven to 375F. Than use a knife to cut off the heard of the garlic cloves. Cut about ¼" from the top. The idea is to expose the inside of every garlic clove, and then drizzle with the oil. Bake for 45 to 50 minutes. The garlic should be sweet and soft. Allow the garlic to cool until you can handle it. Then separate the cloves from the bulb. Mash the cloves in a bowl.

> Mix the lemon juice, mayonnaise, and thyme with the mashed garlic until well combined. Allow it to rest for 15 minutes.

> Cut the sandwich rolls in half and spread the garlic mixture on the inside part of both halves of the rolls. Brush the other side of the bread with olive oil. Put a layer of onions on the bottom half of the roll, then tomatoes, spinach, and then lamb, and top with the other half of the roll.

> Preheat the Cuisinart Griddler to Medium-High with unit closed.

> Cook the sandwiches for 5 minutes, and make sure to check halfway through. The bread should be nicely toasted.

Mint Chili Chutney with Lamb Panini

The lamb gets kicked up a notch in this sandwich. The mint gives it a fresh flavor, and the caramelized onions gives a sweetness that mixes well with the heat of the chutney.

Position: Closed
Selector: Grill/Panini
Plate Side: Grill or Griddle

Prep Time: 20 Minutes
Cook Time: 4 Minutes
Servings: 4

Ingredients:

¾ cup Chili Chutney
2 tsp fresh mint, finely chopped
1 tsp wholegrain mustard
2 tbsps. sour cream or cream cheese
Salt and freshly ground black pepper

4 Panini rolls or olive Ciabatta rolls, cut in half
4-8 slices roast lamb
½ cup caramelized red onion
½ cup feta cheese, crumbled
1½ cup arugula

Directions:

> Combine the chutney, mint, mustard, sour cream, and pepper. Allow it to rest for 15 minutes
> Spread the chutney mixture on the inside part of both halves of the rolls. Brush the other side of the bread with olive oil. Put a layer of onions on the bottom half of the roll, then lamb, arugula, and then feta, and top with the other half of the roll.
> Preheat the Cuisinart Griddler to Medium-High with unit closed.
> Cook the sandwiches for 4 minutes, and make sure to check halfway through. The bread should be nicely toasted, and the cheese should be melted.

Lavish Lamb Panini Burger

The lamb gets a lovely flavor from all the spices. The bread gets nice and crispy thanks to juices and fat released from the lamb as it cooks.

Position: Closed
Selector: Grill/Panini
Plate Side: Grill or Griddle

Prep Time: 10 Minutes
Cook Time: 5 Minutes
Servings: 8

Ingredients:

2 1/2 lbs. ground lamb, preferably shoulder
1 medium onion, very finely chopped
3/4 cup chopped fresh flat-leaf parsley
1 tbsp. ground coriander
3/4 tsp ground cumin

1/2 tsp ground cinnamon
2 tsps. kosher salt
1 1/2 tsps. freshly ground black pepper
1/4 cup olive oil, plus more for grilling
8 thick medium pita breads with pockets

Directions:

> Combine the lamb, oil, and seasoning using a fork. Allow the meat to rest, covered for an hour.

> Open up the pitas and fill them with the lamb mixture. Use the fill the seal the pita.

> Preheat the Cuisinart Griddler to Medium-High with unit closed.

> Cook the sandwiches for 5 minutes, and make sure to check for doneness. The bread should be nicely crunchy, and the lamb is cooked through.

Nothing but the Pork Panini's

Italian Cold Cut Classic Panini

This just like the hoagies you get at an Italian deli. All the flavors meld together so well when they're heated up in and cheese is melted.

Position: Closed
Selector: Grill/Panini
Plate Side: Grill or Griddle

Prep Time: 10 Minutes
Cook Time: 5 Minutes
Servings: 2

Ingredients:

1 12" hoagie roll or the bread of your choice
1 tbsp. olive oil
2 ounces Italian dressing
4 slices provolone cheese
4 slices mortadella

8 slices genoa salami
8 slices deli pepperoni
4 slices tomatoes
2 pepperoncini peppers, chopped

Directions:

> Preheat the Cuisinart Griddler to Medium-High with unit closed.
> Slice the rolls in half and then cut it open.
> Lightly coat the outside of the roll with olive oil using a brush.
> Brush the inside each piece of bread with the dressing. Then top the bottom pieces of bread with cheese. Add the mortadella, salami, tomatoes and pepperoncini's
> Cook the Panini for 5 minutes, checking halfway through. The bread should be brown, and the cheese should be melted.

Pesto Prosciutto Panini

This a great idea if you want a light dinner especially if you serve it with a salad. The saltiness of the prosciutto is balanced out by the fresh herbal flavor of the pesto.

Position: Closed
Selector: Grill/Panini
Plate Side: Grill or Griddle

Prep Time: 10 Minutes
Cook Time: 5 Minutes
Servings: 4

Ingredients:

One 10-ounce loaf Ciabatta, halved horizontally and soft interior removed
1/3 cup Pesto
Extra-virgin olive oil
1/3 lb. Prosciutto de Parma, thinly sliced

Tapenade (optional)
1/4 lb. Fontina cheese, thinly sliced
1/2 cup baby arugula or basil, optional
Coarse salt and fresh ground pepper

Directions:

❯ Preheat the Cuisinart Griddler to Medium-High with unit closed.
❯ Spread pesto on one of the interior sides and olive oil on the other.
❯ Put in a layer of prosciutto, then arugula or basil, then cheese. Top it off with a light drizzle of olive oil and a sprinkle of salt and pepper. Top with the other piece of bread.
❯ Brush the inside each piece of bread with the dressing. Then top the bottom pieces of bread with cheese. Add the mortadella, salami, tomatoes and pepperoncini's
❯ Cook the Panini or 4-5 minutes, checking halfway through. The bread should be brown, and the cheese should be melted.

Prosciutto and Fig Panini

This is a delicious and simple Italian Panini. The saltiness of the prosciutto is balanced out by the sweetness of the figs, and pepperiness of the arugula.

Position: Closed
Selector: Grill/Panini
Plate Side: Grill or Griddle

Prep Time: 10 Minutes
Cook Time: 5 Minutes
Servings: 4

Ingredients:

8 (0.9-ounce) slices crusty
Chicago-style Italian bread
4 ounces very thinly sliced
prosciutto

1 1/4 cups (4 ounces) shredded
Fontina cheese
1/2 cup baby arugula leaves
1/4 cup fig preserves
Olive oil

Directions:

> Preheat the Cuisinart Griddler to Medium-High with unit closed.
> Lightly coat the one side of each piece of bread with olive oil using a brush.
> Spread the fig preserve on 4 pieces of bread (not on the olive oil side). On the other pieces of bread put a layer of prosciutto, then arugula and top with cheese. Place the fig coated bread on top with the fig side touching the cheese.
> Cook the Panini for 5 minutes, checking halfway through. The bread should be brown, and the cheese should be melted.

Salami and Taleggio Panini with Spicy Fennel Honey

This sandwich is so easy to make but delicious. The lovely flavor of the fennel permeates the spicy honey and adds complexity to the salty flavor of the salami.

Position: Closed
Selector: Grill/Panini
Plate Side: Grill or Griddle

Prep Time: 10 Minutes
Cook Time: 5 Minutes
Servings: 6

Ingredients:

1/3 cup honey
1 tbsp. fennel seeds
2 tsps. chili flakes
1/2 loaf focaccia, cut into 4"
squares

1 lb. Taleggio, rind washed, room temperature, thinly sliced
12 slices fennel salami, thinly sliced

Directions:

> Preheat the Cuisinart Griddler to Medium-High with unit closed.
> Put the chili, fennel, and honey in a small saucepan and heat on medium heat. Allow the mixture to cook for 3 to 5 minutes.
> Cut the focaccia in half horizontally. Layer the cheese on one piece of bread and layer the salami on top. Top the salami with a nice drizzle of the honey. Put the other piece of bread on top.
> Brush the inside each piece of bread with the dressing. Then top the bottom pieces of bread with cheese. Add the mortadella, salami, tomatoes and pepperoncini's
> Cook the Panini on for 5 minutes, checking halfway through. The bread should be brown, and the cheese should be melted.
> Top with more honey and serve warm.

Spicy Soppressata Panini with Pesto and Mozzarella

This spicy Italian salami has a great flavor. The mozzarella adds creaminess and the pesto gives a nice herbal flavor.

Position: Closed
Selector: Grill/Panini
Plate Side: Grill or Griddle

Prep Time: 15 Minutes
Cook Time: 5 Minutes
Servings: 4

Ingredients:

1 Ciabatta loaf, cut into 4 portions, or 4 Ciabatta rolls
1/2 cup basil pesto, purchased or homemade

8 ounces fresh mozzarella cheese, sliced
4 ounces sliced spicy Soppressata salami

Directions:

> Preheat the Cuisinart Griddler to Medium-High with unit closed.
> Cut the Ciabatta in half horizontally.
> Spread the pesto on the inside of each piece of bread. Place a layer of salami on the bottom piece of bread and then place the cheese on top. Top with the other piece of bread
> Cook the Panini on for 5 minutes, checking halfway through. The bread should be brown, and the cheese should be melted.

Muffuletta Panini

This sandwich is a classic from the food capital of New Orleans. The olive salad on top and the 3 different types of pork cold cuts make this sandwich unique.

Position: Closed
Selector: Grill/Panini
Plate Side: Grill or Griddle

Prep Time: 10 Minutes
Cook Time: 5 Minutes
Servings: 4

Ingredients:

softened butter
8 slices rustic bread or 8 slices
sourdough bread
16 slices provolone cheese (thin slices) or 16 slices mozzarella cheese (thin slices)

1/2 cup olive salad, drained or
1/2 cup olive tapenade
6 ounces thinly sliced black forest ham
6 ounces sliced mortadella
4 ounces sliced genoa salami

Directions:

> Preheat the Cuisinart Griddler to Medium-High with unit closed.
> Spread butter on both sides of each piece of bread.
> Place 2 pieces of cheese on 4 pieces of bread. Then put down a layer of olive salad, ham, mortadella, salami and top with the remaining cheese. Then top with another piece of bread
> Cook the Panini on medium heat for 5 minutes, checking halfway through. The bread should be brown, and the cheese should be melted.

Bánh Mì Panini

A Bánh Mì a sandwich is a delicious sandwich from Vietnam. It combines delicious French flavors with some Vietnamese flare thanks to the jalapeno and pickled vegetables.

Position: Closed
Selector: Grill/Panini
Plate Side: Grill or Griddle

Prep Time: 10 Minutes
Cook Time: 5 Minutes
Servings: 1

Ingredients:

1 petite baguette roll or 7" section from a regular baguette
Mayonnaise
Maggi Seasoning sauce or light (regular) soy sauce
Liver pâté, boldly flavored cooked pork, sliced and at room temperature

3 or 4 thin, seeded cucumber strips, preferably English
2 or 3 sprigs cilantro, coarsely chopped
3 or 4 thin slices jalapeno chili
1/4 cup Daikon and Carrot Pickle

Directions:

❭ Preheat the Cuisinart Griddler to Medium-High with unit closed.
❭ Cut the bread in half lengthwise. Use your fingers to take out some of the soft part of the middle of both pieces of bread.
❭ Spread the mayonnaise inside both pieces of bread. Lightly coat with the Maggi seasoning sauce, then place the meat on top followed by the cucumbers, cilantro, jalapenos, and then pickles.
❭ Cook the Panini for 5 minutes, checking halfway through. The bread should be nicely toasted.

Bacon Cheddar and Tomato Panini

This melty Panini will have you drooling. The flavors of bacon, cheddar, and tomato, combine to create a delicious All-American flavor.

Position: Closed
Selector: Grill/Panini
Plate Side: Grill or Griddle

Prep Time: 15 Minutes
Cook Time: 5 Minutes
Servings: 4

Ingredients:

4 Roma tomatoes, halved lengthwise, pulp and seeds removed
olive oil
coarse sea salt
fresh ground black pepper

8 basil leaves, thinly sliced
2 tbsps. unsalted butter, melted
8 slices sourdough bread
8 slices bacon, fully cooked
4 ounces sharp cheddar cheese, thinly sliced

Directions:

> Preheat a small skillet on high heat.
> Use a brush to coat the cut side of the tomatoes with olive oil and salt and pepper to taste. Put the tomatoes on the skillet with the cut side down. Allow them to cook for 10 to 12 minutes. The tomatoes. Flip the tomatoes about halfway through. The tomatoes should be wrinkly and the tomatoes should be soft to the touch. Check the tomatoes constantly throughout the process so they don't overcook. Once cooked take them out of the skillet and season with basil.
> Spread the butter on one side of each piece of bread. Place 2 pieces of bacon on the unbuttered side of a piece of bread, then 2 tomatoes and a ¼ of the cheese. Then top with the other piece of bread making sure the butter side is on top.
> Preheat the Cuisinart Griddler to Medium-High with unit closed.
> Cook the Panini for 5 minutes, checking halfway through. The bread should be brown, and the cheese should be melted.

Bacon Mozzarella, Zucchini and Tomato Panini

This is a delicious twist on the BLT. You use grilled Zucchini instead of lettuce, and add in creamy mozzarella for a heavenly sandwich.

Position: Closed
Selector: Grill/Panini
Plate Side: Grill or Griddle

Prep Time: 10 Minutes
Cook Time: 5 Minutes
Servings: 4

Ingredients:

6 slices bacon
1/2 large zucchini, cut lengthwise
into 1/4" slices and grilled
3 tbsp. extra-virgin olive oil,
divided
kosher salt
Freshly ground black pepper

1 medium yellow tomato, thinly
sliced
1 medium red tomato, thinly sliced
1 loaf Ciabatta, halved lengthwise
8 oz. mozzarella, thinly sliced
2 tbsp. Freshly Chopped Basil

Directions:

> Preheat the Cuisinart Griddler to Medium-High with unit closed.
> Put the tomatoes on a plate lined with paper towel in order to soak up any excess liquid.
> Use a brush to coat the inside of the bread with olive oil. Put down a layer of zucchini, then bacon, basil, and finally tomatoes. Salt and pepper to taste and top with top piece of bread. Use a brush to coat the top and bottom of sandwich.
> Spread the butter on one side of each piece of bread. Place 2 pieces of bacon on the unbuttered side of a piece of bread, then 2 tomatoes and a ¼ of the cheese. Then top with another piece of bread making sure the butter side is on top.
> Cook the Panini for 5 minutes, checking halfway through. The bread should be brown, and the cheese should be melted.

Sweet and Salty Bacon Cheesy Panini

This will satisfy your sweet and salt craving all at once. The bacon adds some delicious saltiness to the sweetness of the apple butter.

Position: Closed
Selector: Grill/Panini
Plate Side: Grill or Griddle

Prep Time: 10 Minutes
Cook Time: 3 Minutes
Servings: 4

Ingredients:

8 oz. Brie, thinly sliced
8 pieces thick cut bacon, fully cooked

8 pieces Raisin-walnut bread
½ cup Apple butter
Butter, softened

Directions:

> Preheat the Cuisinart Griddler to Medium-High with unit closed.
> Spread the apple butter on one side of each piece of bread. Then add 2 pieces of bacon to apple butter side of one piece of bread and top with ¼ of the cheese. Place another piece of bread on top with the apple butter side of the bread touching the cheese. Spread butter on the other side of both pieces of bread.
> Cook the Panini for 3 minutes, checking halfway through. The bread should be brown when ready.

Pulsating Poultry Panini's

Bacon Chipotle Chicken Panini

This has everything you need for a heavenly sandwich. The sourdough has a little tartness, the bacon gives it some saltiness, the cheese gives it creaminess, and the chipotle gives it some spice.

Position: Closed
Selector: Grill/Panini
Plate Side: Grill or Griddle

Prep Time: 10 Minutes
Cook Time: 5 Minutes
Servings: 1

Ingredients:

2 slices sourdough bread
1/4 cup Caesar salad dressing
1 cooked chicken breast, diced
1/2 cup shredded Cheddar cheese

1 tbsp. bacon bits
1 1/2 tsps. chipotle chili powder,
or to taste
2 tbsps. softened butter

Directions:

> Preheat the Cuisinart Griddler to Medium-High with unit closed.
> Spread the salad dressing on one side of both pieces of bread. Then top the dressing side of one piece of bread with chicken, then cheese, then bacon, and finally chipotle chili powder. Place the other piece of bread with the dressing side down on top. Butter the other side of both pieces of bread.
> Cook the Panini for 5 minutes, checking halfway through. The bread should be brown, and the cheese should be melted.

Buffalo Chicken Panini

This Panini is an easy way to get your buffalo wings fix. The onions give a little bit of sweetness and the cheese helps to balance out spice from the buffalo sauce.

Position: Closed
Selector: Grill/Panini
Plate Side: Grill or Griddle

Prep Time: 30 Minutes
Cook Time: 4 Minutes
Servings: 4

Ingredients:

2 cups shredded cooked chicken
1 large sweet onion, sliced
8 slices seedless rye
1/4 lb. thinly sliced Swiss cheese,
about 8 slices

1/4 cup blue cheese dressing
1 cup mayonnaise
1 cup buffalo hot sauce
2 tbsps. unsalted butter
blue cheese dressing

Directions:

> Melt the butter in a large skillet on medium heat. Add the onions and cook for about 20 minutes.

> Mix the buffalo sauce and mayonnaise in a medium bowl and toss with the chicken.

> Put a slice of cheese on a piece of bread then the chicken, the onions and top with another slice of cheese and top with another piece of bread. Repeat the process with the remaining sandwiches. Spread the butter on the top and bottom of the sandwich

> Preheat the Cuisinart Griddler to Medium-High with unit closed.

> Cook the sandwiches for 4 minutes, and make sure to check halfway through. The bread should be brown, and the cheese should be melted. Serve the sandwiches with a side of the blue cheese dressing.

Spinach and Pesto Chicken Panini

This is a delicious light and fresh sandwich. The spinach gives the sandwich a nice crunch, the pesto gives a jolt of flavor and cheese provides some gooey creaminess.

Position: Closed
Selector: Grill/Panini
Plate Side: Grill or Griddle

Prep Time: 10 Minutes
Cook Time: 5 Minutes
Servings: 1

Ingredients:

1/2 cup mayonnaise
2 tbsps. prepared pesto
1 1/2 cups shredded rotisserie chicken
Kosher salt
Freshly ground pepper

1 1lb. Ciabatta loaf, split lengthwise and cut into 4 pieces
Extra-virgin olive oil, for brushing
1 cup lightly packed baby spinach
8 thin slices of Swiss cheese

Directions:

> Preheat the Cuisinart Griddler to Medium-High with unit closed.
> Use a whisk to combine the pesto and mayonnaise. Then mix in the chicken and salt and pepper to taste.
> Use a brush to coat the top and bottom of the bread with olive oil. Put a layer of chicken on the bottom piece of bread, then spinach, and finally cheese. Place the top piece of bread on the cheese.
> Cook the sandwiches for 5 minutes, and make sure to check halfway through. The bread should be brown, and the cheese should be melted.

Dijon and Berry Chicken Panini

This has a beautiful mix of sweet and spicy. The blackberries pair so well with the mustard, and peppery flavor of the arugula.

Position: Closed
Selector: Grill/Panini
Plate Side: Grill or Griddle

Prep Time: 15 Minutes
Cook Time: 5 Minutes
Servings: 1

Ingredients:

4 Bakery Ciabatta rolls or French hamburger buns
2 tbsps. herb garlic butter, melted
1/3 cup fresh blackberries (about 6 berries)
1 tbsp. honey
1/2 cup stone-ground mustard

3.5 oz. Deli aged white cheddar cheese, shredded
1 medium red onion, coarsely chopped
1 cup fresh baby arugula, coarsely chopped
1 Deli rotisserie chicken, shredded

Directions:

> Preheat the Cuisinart Griddler to Medium-High with unit closed.
> Slice the rolls in half horizontally. Mash the berries in a bowl and mix with the honey and then mix in the mustard. In a separate bowl mix together the chicken, arugula, cheese, and onions.
> Spread butter on the outside of the bread. Spread the berry mixture on the inside of the bread. Put chicken mixture on the inside of the bottom piece of bread, and place the top piece of bread on the chicken.
> Cook the sandwiches for 5 minutes, and make sure to check halfway through. The bread should be brown, and the cheese should be melted.

Chicken Portobello Panini

This is a delicious and simple Panini. The Portobello adds a lovely earthiness to chicken, and the tomatoes add some freshness.

Position: Closed
Selector: Grill/Panini
Plate Side: Grill or Griddle

Prep Time: 15 Minutes
Cook Time: 5 Minutes
Servings: 4

Ingredients:

1 tbsp. olive oil
1 tbsp. red wine vinegar
1/2 tsp Italian Seasoning Mix
1/2 tsp salt
1/4 tsp coarsely ground black pepper
1 garlic clove, pressed
2 large Portobello mushroom caps

2 slices (1/2" thick) large white onion
1 cup (4 ounces) grated Provolone cheese
2 plum tomatoes, sliced
8 slices (3/4" thick) Italian bread
1 cup shredded roasted chicken

Directions:

❭ Preheat a skillet on medium heat for 5 minutes. Then place the onions and the mushrooms in the skillet. Allow them to cook for about 4 to 6 minutes, making sure to flip halfway through. Cut the onions in half and the mushrooms into thin slices.

❭ Brush what's going to be the outside of the bread with olive oil. Top half the pieces of bread with a layer cheese, then, chicken, then mushrooms, then onions, then tomatoes, and a second layer of cheese. Top with another piece of bread making sure the olive oil side is on the outside.

❭ Preheat the Cuisinart Griddler to Medium-High with unit closed.

❭ Cook the sandwiches for 5 minutes, and make sure to flip halfway through. The bread should be brown, and the cheese should be melted.

Bruschetta Turkey Panini

This is a great way to get all the flavor of bruschetta in sandwich form. The turkey's light flavor allows, the basil, tomatoes, and mozzarella to shine.

Position: Closed
Selector: Grill/Panini
Plate Side: Grill or Griddle

Prep Time: 10 Minutes
Cook Time: 5 Minutes
Servings: 4

Ingredients:

8 slices Italian bread
8 fresh basil leaves
8 thinly sliced tomatoes
16 slices of Black Pepper Turkey Breast

4 pieces of mozzarella cheese
4 tbsps. mayonnaise
Olive oil

Directions:

> Preheat the Cuisinart Griddler to Medium-High with unit closed.
> Cut the basil into ribbons.
> Place a layer of turkey on a piece of bread, then basil, and then cheese. Spread the mayo on the bottom part of the top piece of bread, and place it on top of the cheese. Brush the top and bottom of the sandwich with olive oil
> Cook the sandwiches for 5 minutes, and make sure to flip halfway through. The bread should be brown, and the cheese should be melted.

Southwestern Turkey Panini

This sandwich is packed will all sorts of southwestern flavor. The chipotle mayo gives it a kick, the avocado gives it creaminess, and the Colby jack cheese gives it a depth of flavor.

Position: Closed
Selector: Grill/Panini
Plate Side: Grill or Griddle

Prep Time: 15 Minutes
Cook Time: 5 Minutes
Servings: 4

Ingredients:

1 medium Avocado peeled and seeded
½ tbsp. Cilantro leaves finely chopped
½ tsp Lime juice
Salt to taste

Chipotle mayonnaise (store bought or homemade)
4 slices large Sourdough bread
8 slices Colby Jack Cheese
8 slices Blackened Oven Roasted Turkey Breast
4 slices Tomato

Directions:
> Preheat the Cuisinart Griddler to Medium-High with unit closed.
> Mash and mix the avocado, lime and cilantro, and then salt and pepper to taste.
> Spread the chipotle mayonnaise on one side of every piece of bread. On 2 pieces of bread with the mayonnaise side facing up place a layer of cheese, then turkey, then tomato, then avocado mixture, then turkey, and finally cheese again. Top with another piece of bread with the mayonnaise side touching the cheese.
> Cook the sandwiches for 5 minutes, and make sure to check halfway through. The bread should be toasted, and the cheese should be melted.

Smoked Provolone and Turkey Panini

This simple sandwich has a world of flavors in it. The provolone gives it a nice Smokey flavor which, works well with the spiciness of the Dijon, and the creaminess of the mayonnaise.

Position: Closed
Selector: Grill/Panini
Plate Side: Grill or Griddle

Prep Time: 5 Minutes
Cook Time: 5 Minutes
Servings: 4

Ingredients:

1 round Asiago Cheese Focaccia
3 tbsps. light mayonnaise
2 tsps. Dijon mustard
5 ounces thinly sliced smoked
provolone

8 ounces thinly sliced smoked
turkey breast
1 ripe beefsteak tomato, thinly
sliced
1 ounce baby spinach leaves
Olive oil

Directions:

> Preheat the Cuisinart Griddler to Medium-High with unit closed.
> Cut the bread in half horizontally.
> Spread a layer of mayonnaise and a layer of mustard on the inside of the top piece of bread. Place a layer of turkey on the inside of the bottom piece of bread then, spinach, then tomatoes, and top with cheese. Place the top piece of bread on the cheese with the mayonnaise side down. If necessary cut the sandwiches into wedges in order to fit it in your flip sandwich maker.
> Cook the sandwiches for 5 to 6 minutes, and make sure to check halfway through. The bread should be toasted, and the cheese should be melted. Cut the sandwiches into 4 wedges if you haven't already done so.

The Ultimate Thanksgiving Reuben Panini

This is a great way to use your thanksgiving leftovers. The addition of cranberries to the Russian dressing makes this particular festive along with the substitution of turkey for corned beef.

Position: Closed
Selector: Grill/Panini
Plate Side: Grill or Griddle

Prep Time: 7 Minutes
Cook Time: 5 Minutes
Servings: 4

Ingredients:

1/3 cup mayonnaise
2 tbsps. cranberry sauce (I used whole berry)
2 tsps. freshly grated horseradish
1 tsp Worcestershire sauce
Kosher salt and black pepper, to taste

2 cups shredded green cabbage or packaged Cole slaw
8 slices rye bread
8 slices Swiss cheese
3/4 lb. carved turkey, thinly sliced
2 tbsps. melted butter

Directions:

> Preheat the Cuisinart Griddler to Medium-High with unit closed.

> Mix together the first 4 ingredients using a whisk. Salt and pepper to taste. Combine the mixture with the cabbage until well coated.

> Put a layer of cheese, then turkey, a layer of the slaw, another layer of turkey, and another layer of cheese on a piece of bread. Top with another piece of bread. Spread the butter on the top and bottom of the sandwich

> Cook the sandwiches for 5 minutes, and make sure to check halfway through. The bread should be toasted, and the cheese should be melted.

The Thanksgiving Turkey Cuban Panini

This is another recipe that puts your thanksgiving leftovers to good use. This take on the famous Cuban sandwich adds cranberries to the Dijon mayonnaise and adds turkey to the traditional pork.

Position: Closed
Selector: Grill/Panini
Plate Side: Grill or Griddle

Prep Time: 15 Minutes
Cook Time: 5 Minutes
Servings: 4

Ingredients:

2 tbsps. mayonnaise
2 tbsps. Dijon mustard
2 tbsps. leftover cranberry sauce
Salt and freshly ground black pepper
4 slices good quality Italian bread
4 slices Swiss cheese

2 slices cooked ham
6 slices leftover cooked turkey
8 dill pickle slices
Olive oil

Directions:

❯ Preheat the Cuisinart Griddler to Medium-High with unit closed.
❯ Mix together the first mayonnaise, cranberry sauce, and Dijon mustard using a whisk. Salt and pepper to taste. Combine the mixture with the cabbage until well coated.
❯ Spread a layer of the newly made cranberry Dijon sauce on what's going to be the inside of 2 pieces of bread. Put a layer of cheese, then turkey, a layer of the ham, a layer of pickles, and another layer of cheese on the pieces of bread. Top with another piece of bread. Brush the top and bottom of the sandwich with olive oil
❯ Cook the sandwiches for 5 minutes, and make sure to check halfway through. The bread should be toasted, and the cheese should be melted. Once you're ready to serve, slice the sandwiches in half.

Healthy Veggie "No Meat" Panini's

Corn and Zucchini Pepper Jack Panini

This Panini is perfect for summer when you can get lots of zucchini and sweet corn. The pepper jack gives this sandwich some heat which is balanced out by the sweetness of the corn. The zucchini gives it a nice crunch

Position: Closed
Selector: Grill/Panini
Plate Side: Grill or Griddle

Prep Time: 10 Minutes
Cook Time: 5 Minutes
Servings: 4

Ingredients:

1 tbsp. olive oil
1 large clove garlic, minced
1 ear corn, kernels removed
1 small zucchini, quartered
lengthwise and sliced

Salt + pepper to taste
8 slices bread
2 tbsp. butter, softened
1 cup shredded pepper jack cheese

Directions:

> Place the oil in a skillet and heat it on medium high heat. Cook the garlic in the oil for about 15 seconds, until it's fragrant. Mix in the corn and zucchini and cook for around 3 minutes. The zucchini should be soft but not mushy. Remove the mixture from the heat and salt and pepper to taste.

> Place a layer of cheese on 4 pieces of bread, then the vegetable mixture, and then another layer of cheese. Top with the remaining slices of bread. Butter both the top and bottom of the sandwich.

> Preheat the Cuisinart Griddler to High with unit closed.

> Cook the Panini for 5 to 6 minutes, checking halfway through. The bread should be brown, and the cheese should be melted.

Lemony Delicious Summer Vegetable Panini

This Panini has all the bounty of summer, and a nice light lemony flavor. It's the perfect light summer lunch filled with vegetables and creamy ricotta cheese.

Position: Closed
Selector: Grill/Panini
Plate Side: Grill or Griddle

Prep Time: 15 Minutes
Cook Time: 5 Minutes
Servings: 4

Ingredients:

1 tbsps. olive oil
1 small onion, sliced
1 medium yellow squash, thinly sliced
1 medium zucchini, thinly sliced
1 red bell pepper, sliced
2 tsps. of lemon zest
¼ tsp salt

4 Ciabatta rolls or 4 pieces of focaccia
1/8 tsp ground black pepper
1 cup part-skim ricotta cheese
2 tsps. lemon zest
1 ½ tsps. lemon juice
1/8 tsp salt
1/8 tsp ground black pepper

Directions:

> Place the oil in a skillet and heat it on medium high heat. Cook the onions in the oil for about 3 to 4 seconds, until they start to soften. Mix in the squash, peppers and zucchini and cook for another 5 to 7 minutes. Mix in the first 2 tsps. of lemon zest and 1/8 tsp of pepper and the ¼ tsp of salt. Remove the mixture from the heat and set aside in a bowl.
> Mix the last 5 ingredients in a bowl.
> Slice the rolls in half horizontally and place a layer of the ricotta mixture on the inside of each piece of bread.
> Place the vegetable mixture on the bottom pieces of bread. Pot the top pieces of bread on the vegetables, making sure the ricotta side is touching the vegetables.
> Preheat the Cuisinart Griddler to Medium-High with unit closed.
> Cook the Panini for 4 to 5 minutes, checking halfway through. The bread should be brown, and the cheese should be melted.

Provolone Baby Mushroom and Caramelized Onion Panini

This Panini is the closest thing you're going to get to French onion soup in sandwich form. The caramelized onions are just like the onions found in French onion soup, and your bread mimics the delicious top of the soup. The mushrooms sop up all the delicious caramelized onion flavor and add a light earthiness.

Position: Closed
Selector: Grill/Panini
Plate Side: Grill or Griddle

Prep Time: 40 Minutes
Cook Time: 5 Minutes
Servings: 5

Ingredients:

2 tbsps. unsalted butter
2 tbsps. olive oil
1 and 1/2 large onions (or 2 medium) sliced into 1/4" thick slices
1 tbsp. sugar
1/4 tsp thyme
2 tbsps. minced garlic (I used 1 and 1/2)
1 tsp Worcestershire sauce
8 oz. fresh baby Bella mushrooms, sliced into 1/4" thick slices

1/2 tsp black pepper
salt to taste
1/4 - 1/2 tsp red pepper flakes (or more to taste)
1 tsp flour
1/4 cup mushroom broth (or beef broth)
2 tbsps. minced parsley
5 - 1 oz. slices provolone cheese, cut in half
10 slices of fresh French bread
Olive oil

Directions:

> Heat a big skillet on medium heat, making sure it's hot before adding any ingredients. Put in the olive oil and butter, and allow the butter to melt. Then put in the onions and allow them to cook for 5 minutes. Mix in the sugar and cook for an additional 15 minutes. Mix in the Worcester sauce, garlic, and thyme, and allow the mixture to cook for 2 more minutes before mixing in the mushrooms. Cook for 10 minutes before mixing in the red and black pepper along with the flour. Slowly mix in the broth 1 tbsp. at a time, waiting until it's been absorbed before adding another. After you've added all of the

broth and it's been absorbed, remove it from the heat and mix in the parsley.

> Place a layer of cheese on 5 pieces of bread, then the vegetable mixture, and then another layer of cheese. Top with the remaining slices of bread. Brush the olive oil on both the top and bottom of the sandwiches.

> Preheat the Cuisinart Griddler to Medium-High with unit closed.

> Cook the Panini for 3 to 4 minutes, cooking halfway through. The bread should be toasted, and the cheese should be melted.

Hummus and Vegetable Panini

This Panini is incredibly easy to make, and so light and fresh. It's packed with wholesome vegetable, and delicious hummus.

Position: Closed
Selector: Grill/Panini
Plate Side: Grill or Griddle

Prep Time: 10 Minutes
Cook Time: 5 Minutes
Servings: 4

Ingredients:

1 tbsps. olive oil
1 small onion, sliced
1 medium zucchini, thinly sliced
1 medium cucumber, thinly sliced
1 red bell pepper, sliced
8 slices whole grain bread

4 tbsp. homemade or store-bought
hummus of your choice
fresh spinach leaves
1 cup matchstick carrots
slice of provolone cheese

Directions:

❯ Preheat the Cuisinart Griddler to Medium-High with unit closed.
❯ Spread the hummus on 1 side of 4 pieces of bread. Layer the vegetables starting with the zucchini, then, cucumber, then spinach then red bell pepper, then carrots. Top the vegetables with a slice of cheese and place another piece of bread on the cheese. Brush the top and bottom of the sandwich with olive oil
❯ Cook the Panini or 4 to 5 minutes, checking halfway through. The bread should be brown, and the cheese should be melted.

Shaved Asparagus and Balsamic Cherries with Pistachios Panini

This Panini is a strange mix of flavor combinations. I'm sure you would never think to put cherries and asparagus together but they work.

Position: Closed
Selector: Grill/Panini
Plate Side: Grill or Griddle

Prep Time: 15 Minutes
Cook Time: 5 Minutes
Servings: 4

Ingredients:

1 to 1 and 1/2 cups pitted, chopped Bing cherries
zest from 2 lemons
3 to 4 tbsp. balsamic vinegar
roughly 1/2 bunch of thick-stalk asparagus, shaved with a mandolin or vegetable peeler
2 tbsp. fresh mint, thinly sliced

2 tbsp. fresh basil, thinly sliced
2 tbsp. pistachio oil
1 multigrain baguette, cut in half, and split open
ricotta
fresh mozzarella
salt and freshly-cracked pepper
1/2 tbsp. butter, softened

Directions:

> Preheat the Cuisinart Griddler to Medium-High with unit closed.
> Mix the cherries, balsamic vinegar, and lemon zest. Then salt and pepper to taste.
> Mix the asparagus mint, pistachio oil, and basil in a separate bowl.
> Cut the mozzarella into slices that are 1/3" thick. Place them on the inside part of the pieces of bread and place the cherry mixture on top of it. Then place the asparagus mixture on top of that
> Use a knife top spread the ricotta on the inside of the top pieces of bread, and place it on the asparagus mixture.
> Cook the Panini for 5 to 6 minutes, checking halfway through. The bread should be brown, and the cheese should appear to be melted.
> Cut the sandwiches in half before serving.

Avocado and Mixed Vegetable Panini

This Panini is so delicious and creamy thanks to the cheese and avocado. The sautéed vegetable is packed with flavor and all sorts of good vitamins and minerals.

Position: Closed
Selector: Grill/Panini
Plate Side: Grill or Griddle

Prep Time: 15 Minutes
Cook Time: 5 Minutes
Servings: 4

Ingredients:

1 1/2 tbsps. butter or olive oil
1 minced shallot (onion or garlic works too)
8 ounces sliced baby Portobello mushrooms
1 cup cherry or grape tomatoes
2 cups chopped kale, stems removed

salt to taste
2 avocados
8 pieces thick, sturdy wheat bread
White cheese like Provolone or Mozzarella
Olive oil

Directions:

❯ Put the butter in a big skillet and allow it to melt on medium heat. Put in the shallots and cook until they become translucent. Mix in the mushrooms, and cook until they start to brown. Then mix in the kale and tomatoes, and cook until the kale wilts, and the tomatoes are cooked through.

❯ Mash the avocados using a fork. Spread the avocado on what's going to be the inside of each piece of bread. Then place a layer of cheese on half of the pieces of bread, then a layer of veggies, and finally another layer of cheese. Top with another piece of bread. Brush the top and bottom of the sandwich with olive oil.

❯ Preheat the Cuisinart Griddler to Medium-High with unit closed.

❯ Cook the Panini for 4 to 5 minutes, checking halfway through. The bread should be brown, and the cheese should be melted.

Thai Peanut Peach Panini with Basil

This makes a delicious and unexpected dessert. The sweetness of the peaches is well paired by the creaminess of the peanut sauce, and the aromatic flavor of the basil.

Position: Closed
Selector: Grill/Panini
Plate Side: Grill or Griddle

Prep Time: 10 Minutes
Cook Time: 5 Minutes
Servings: 1

Ingredients:

2 tbsp. creamy natural peanut butter
1 tbsp. agave or maple syrup
1/2 tbsp. soy sauce or tamari
1/2 tbsp. lime juice
2 slices good sandwich bread

1 small or 1/2 large peach sliced thin
2 tbsp. fresh basil leaves
1-2 tsp. olive oil
Butter, softened

Directions:

❯ Preheat the Cuisinart Griddler to Medium-High with unit closed.
❯ Mix together the first 4 ingredients using a whisk. If the sauce is too thick you can thin it out with a small amount of water. The sauce will natural thin when it's grilled.
❯ Spread a large amount of the peanut sauce on what's going to be the inside pieces of bread. Layer the peaches and basil on the peanut sauce side of one of the pieces of bread, and then top with the other. Spread the butter on the top and bottom of the sandwich
❯ Cook the Panini for 3 to 5 minutes, checking halfway through. The bread should be brown, and the cheese should be melted.

Vegan Pepper Jack Roasted Pepper Panini

This spicy sandwich will hit the spot for any vegan. The peppers provide a world of flavor, the vegan cheese adds creaminess, and the Harissa adds some lovely heat.

Position: Closed
Selector: Grill/Panini
Plate Side: Grill or Griddle

Prep Time: 10 Minutes
Cook Time: 5 Minutes
Servings: 1

Ingredients:

2 slices bread (sourdough used)
2 tsp. vegan buttery spread
5 thin slices of tomato
1/4 cup (handful) of fresh basil leaves

1/4 - 1/3 cup vegan pepper jack cheese shreds such as Daiya
2-3 thin slices roasted red or yellow pepper
1/2 cup baby spinach
pinches of black pepper
1 tbsp. Harissa

Directions:

> Preheat the Cuisinart Griddler to Medium-High with unit closed.
> Spread what's going to be the outside of each piece of bread with the vegan buttery spread. Spread the Harissas on what's going to be the inside of each piece of bread.
> Place the tomatoes on one of the pieces of bread, then the spinach, then the basil, then the peppers, and top with the vegan cheese. Place the other piece of bread on top with the Harissa touching the cheese.
> Cook the Panini for 3 to 5 minutes, checking halfway through. The bread should be brown, and the cheese should be melted.

Peach Caprese Panini

This is like having a delightful caprese salad with a sweet twist. The peach gives it a delightful sweetness that's balanced by the creamy mozzarella, the aromatic flavor of the basil, and the tartness of the balsamic vinegar. Try using burrata instead of mozzarella for even more creaminess

Position: Closed
Selector: Grill/Panini
Plate Side: Grill or Griddle

Prep Time: 10 Minutes
Cook Time: 5 Minutes
Servings: 1

Ingredients:
1 French deli roll, split
1 ½ tsp balsamic vinegar
2 slices mozzarella cheese
1 small heirloom tomato, sliced

4 fresh basil leaves
olive oil
1 small peach, sliced

Directions:
> Preheat the Cuisinart Griddler to Medium-High with unit closed.
> Sprinkle the balsamic vinegar on the inside of both pieces of bread. Brush the outside of both pieces of bread with olive oil
> Place one of the mozzarella slices on the bottom piece of bread, then the peaches, then the tomatoes, and top with the other piece of cheese. Place the other piece of bread on top of the cheese.
> Cook the Panini for 5 minutes, checking halfway through. The bread should be toasted, and the cheese should be melted.

Ratatouille Panini

This is a take on the classic French dish. It makes for a delicious, healthy vegetarian sandwich that's perfect for lunch. The roasted red pepper sauce gives it a lot of flavor.

Position: Closed
Selector: Grill/Panini
Plate Side: Grill or Griddle

Prep Time: 20 Minutes
Cook Time: 5 Minutes
Servings: 1

Ingredients:

1 red bell pepper, sliced
1 tomato, chopped
1 clove garlic, minced
1 tsp dried oregano, or to taste
salt and ground black pepper to taste
1 eggplant, sliced

1 zucchini, sliced
1 tomato, sliced
1 red onion, sliced
4 tsps. olive oil
4 slices sourdough bread
4 slices mozzarella cheese

Directions:

> Warm a skillet on high heat, and place the red bell pepper in it for around 5 minutes. The pepper should be soft when it's ready. Place the red pepper, chopped tomato, garlic in a blender or food processor. Blend or process until a smooth sauce is formed. Add salt, pepper, and oregano to taste.

> Grill the remaining vegetable on a grille or the same skillet for about 6 minutes flipping halfway through. The vegetables will be soft when ready.

> Brush what's going to be the outside of the bread slices with olive oil. Spread the sauce on what's going to be the inside of the bread. Layer a piece of piece of cheese on 2 of the pieces of bread, then the vegetable mixture, then another piece of cheese. Top with another piece of bread with the sauce side touching the cheese.

> Preheat the Cuisinart Griddler to Medium-High with unit closed.

> Cook the Panini for 4 to 5 minutes, checking halfway through. The bread should be toasted, and the cheese should be melted.

123

Anytime Breakfast Panini's

Bacon Egg and Sausage Breakfast Panini

This Panini is perfect for all meat lovers. It's packed with so much flavor thanks to the meat, cheese, bell pepper, and pesto. It's so good you might want 2!

Position: Closed
Selector: Grill/Panini
Plate Side: Grill or Griddle

Prep Time: 20 Minutes
Cook Time: 6 Minutes
Servings: 2

Ingredients:

2 pita breads
1/2cup pesto
2 eggs
1 cup shredded sharp cheddar cheese
1 cup shredded Monterey Jack cheese
1 cup shredded mozzarella cheese

1 pork sausage patty, cooked
2 strips bacon, cooked
1/3 cup roasted red pepper
1-2 tbsps. butter, melted
2 scallions, chopped

Directions:

> Use a whisk to beat the egg with a pinch of salt and pepper. Place the butter in a skillet and melt it on medium heat. Use a spoon to stir the eggs and push them across the pan. Cook until the eggs set, about 1 to 2 minutes.

> Chop the sausage into small pieces. Spread the pesto on half of both pieces of pita. Top the pitas with half the cheese, then eggs, bacon, sausage, bell pepper, the remaining, cheese and then top with the scallions. Fold the other side of the pita on top of the filling and spread the butter on the outside of the pitas.

> Preheat the Cuisinart Griddler to Medium-High with unit closed.

> Cook the Panini for 4 to 6 minutes, checking halfway through. The bread should be brown, and the cheese should be melted.

French Toast and Grilled Banana Panini

This Panini is a banana lover's dream. The perfectly caramelized bananas are only enhanced by the wonderful flavor of the French toast, creating a sandwich everyone in your family will love!

Position: Closed
Selector: Grill/Panini
Plate Side: Grill or Griddle

Prep Time: 20 Minutes
Cook Time: 6 Minutes
Servings: 4

Ingredients:

6 large eggs
1 cup whole milk
1/2 cup heavy cream
1/4 cup fresh orange juice
2 tbsps. vanilla extract
2 tbsps. cognac (optional)
2 tbsps. granulated sugar
1/2 tsp ground cinnamon
Pinch of freshly grated nutmeg

Salt
8 slices Texas toast or other thick white bread
3 large ripe bananas
2 tbsps. unsalted butter, melted
Confectioners' sugar, for garnish
Pure maple syrup, for garnish

Directions:

> Use a whisk to combine the eggs, milk, cream, orange juice, cognac, sugar, cinnamon, and vanilla. Put the bread in a couple of shallow baking dishes and cover with the mixture you just created. Allow the bread to rest in the mixture for 10 minutes
> While the bread is resting preheat a skillet on medium heat. Then coat the bananas with melted butter and cook them in the skillet until are nice and brown all over, about 3 minutes. They should be releasing their juices. When bananas have cooled down a little chop them into chunks.
> Preheat the Cuisinart Griddler to Medium-High with unit closed.
> While that's preheating place the bananas on half the pieces of bread and top with the other pieces of bread.
> Cook the Panini for 6 minutes in your preheated griddle, checking halfway through.
> Top with confectioners' sugar and maple syrup

Chocolate Hazelnut French Toast Panini

This Panini has a beautiful flavor profile. The richness of the chocolate hazelnut spread provides some richness to the sweetness of the French toast, and the hazelnuts provide a perfect crunch in contrast to the soft inside of the French toast!

Position: Closed
Selector: Grill/Panini
Plate Side: Grill or Griddle

Prep Time: 20 Minutes
Cook Time: 6 Minutes
Servings: 4

Ingredients:

6 large eggs
1 cup whole milk
1/2 cup heavy cream
1/4 cup fresh orange juice (from about 1 medium orange)
2 tbsps. vanilla extract
2 tbsps. cognac (optional)
2 tbsps. granulated sugar
1/2 tsp ground cinnamon

Pinch of freshly grated nutmeg
Salt
8 slices Texas toast or other thick white bread
½ cup hazelnut spread with cocoa
¼ cup chopped hazelnuts, toasted
Confectioners' sugar, for garnish
Pure maple syrup, for garnish

Directions:

❯ Spread the hazelnut spread on 4 of the pieces of bread and then place the hazelnuts on top. Top with the pieces of bread.
❯ Use a whisk to combine the eggs, milk, cream, orange juice, cognac, sugar, cinnamon, and vanilla. Put the sandwiches in a shallow baking dishes and cover with the mixture you just created. Allow the sandwiches to rest in the mixture for 10 min.
❯ Preheat the Cuisinart Griddler to Medium-High with unit closed.
❯ Cook the Panini on medium for 6 minutes, checking halfway through.
❯ Top with confectioners' sugar and maple syrup

French Toast and Strawberries in Cream Panini

This Panini will a huge hit with your kids. The cream cheese mixes perfectly with the strawberries as a delicious surprise in the middle of two delicious pieces of French toast!

Position: Closed
Selector: Grill/Panini
Plate Side: Grill or Griddle

Prep Time: 20 Minutes
Cook Time: 6 Minutes
Servings: 4

Ingredients:

6 large eggs
1 cup whole milk
1/2 cup heavy cream
1/4 cup fresh orange juice (from about 1 medium orange)
2 tbsps. vanilla extract
2 tbsps. cognac (optional)
2 tbsps. granulated sugar
1/2 tsp ground cinnamon
Pinch of freshly grated nutmeg

Salt
8 slices Texas toast or other thick white bread
1/2 cup cream cheese
1/2 cup of strawberries, sliced thinly + 1/4 cup strawberries cut into small pieces
Confectioners' sugar, for garnish
Pure maple syrup, for garnish

Directions:

> Spread the cream cheese on what's going to be the inside of the pieces of bread and then place the strawberries on top of 4 of them. Top with the remaining pieces of bread.
> Use a whisk to combine the eggs, milk, cream, orange juice, cognac, sugar, cinnamon, and vanilla. Put the sandwiches in a shallow baking dishes and cover with the mixture you just created. Allow the sandwiches to rest in the mixture for 10 min.
> Preheat the Cuisinart Griddler to Medium-High with unit closed.
> Cook the Panini for 6 to 7 minutes, checking halfway through.
> Top with confectioners' sugar and maple syrup

Mixed Berry French Toast Panini

This Panini has all the berry flavor you can handle. The creaminess of the cream cheese enhances the flavors of the raspberries and blackberries. Use frozen berries if you can't find fresh ones, but make sure to thaw them out first.

Position: Closed
Selector: Grill/Panini
Plate Side: Grill or Griddle

Prep Time: 20 Minutes
Cook Time: 6 Minutes
Servings: 4

Ingredients:

6 large eggs
1 cup whole milk
1/2 cup heavy cream
1/4 cup fresh orange juice (from about 1 medium orange)
2 tbsps. vanilla extract
2 tbsps. cognac (optional)
2 tbsps. granulated sugar
1/2 tsp ground cinnamon

Pinch of freshly grated nutmeg
Pinch of salt
8 slices Texas toast or other thick white bread
1 cup blackberries
1 cup raspberries
Confectioners' sugar, for garnish
Pure maple syrup, for garnish

Directions:

> Spread the cream cheese on what's going to be the inside of the pieces of bread and then place the strawberries on top of 4 of them. Top with the remaining pieces of bread.
> Use a whisk to combine the eggs, milk, cream, orange juice, cognac, sugar, cinnamon, and vanilla. Put the sandwiches in a shallow baking dishes and cover with the mixture you just created. Allow sandwiches to rest in the mixture for 10 minutes.
> Preheat the Cuisinart Griddler to Medium-High with unit closed.
> Cook the Panini for 6 minutes, checking halfway through.
> Top with confectioners' sugar and maple syrup.

Spicy Chocolate Hazelnut Bacon French Toast Panini

So many delicious layers of flavor here. Delicious nuttiness from the chocolate hazelnut spread, heat from the cayenne, and bacon. Yumm!

Position: Closed
Selector: Grill/Panini
Plate Side: Grill or Griddle

Prep Time: 20 Minutes
Cook Time: 6 Minutes
Servings: 4

Ingredients:

6 large eggs
1 cup whole milk
1/2 cup heavy cream
1/4 cup fresh orange juice (from about 1 medium orange)
2 tbsps. vanilla extract
2 tbsps. cognac (optional)
2 tbsps. granulated sugar
1/2 tsp ground cinnamon
Pinch of freshly grated nutmeg

Pinch of salt
Cayenne Pepper
8 strips of bacon, cooked
8 slices Texas toast or other thick white bread
½ cup hazelnut spread with cocoa
¼ cup chopped hazelnuts, toasted
Confectioners' sugar, for garnish
Pure maple syrup, for garnish

Directions:

> Spread the hazelnut spread on 4 of the pieces of bread and then place the bacon on top. Add cayenne pepper to taste. Top with the pieces of bread.
> Use a whisk to combine the eggs, milk, cream, orange juice, cognac, sugar, cinnamon, and vanilla. Put the sandwiches in a shallow baking dishes and cover with the mixture you just created. Allow the sandwiches to rest in the mixture for 10 minutes.
> Preheat the Cuisinart Griddler to Medium-High with unit closed.
> Cook the Panini for 6 minutes, checking halfway through.
> Top with confectioners' sugar and maple syrup

Prosciutto and Egg Bagel Panini

This Panini is great for breakfast sandwich and bagel lovers. The prosciutto adds a nice saltiness to the cheese, and the rich flavor of the eggs. Use your favorite bagel to make it special!

Position: Closed
Selector: Grill/Panini
Plate Side: Grill or Griddle

Prep Time: 10 Minutes
Cook Time: 3 Minutes
Servings: 2

Ingredients:

2 eggs
2 everything bagels (or any favorite bagel)
2 tbsps. mayonnaise
2 slices American cheese
4 slices prosciutto

2 handfuls baby arugula
Kosher salt
Ground black pepper
Olive oil
2 tsp butter

Directions:

❯ Use a whisk to beat the egg with a pinch of salt and pepper. Place the butter in a skillet and melt it on medium heat. Use a spoon to stir the eggs and push them across the pan. Cook until the eggs set, about 1 to 20 minutes.

❯ Cut the bagels in half horizontally. Spread the mayonnaise on the inside of the bagel. Layer the eggs, on the inside of 2 of the bagel halves, then the cheese, then the arugula, then the prosciutto. Top with the remaining pieces of bagel. Brush the top and bottom of the sandwiches with olive oil.

❯ Preheat the Cuisinart Griddler to Medium-High with unit closed.

❯ Cook the Panini for 2 to 3 minutes, checking halfway through. The bagels should be toasted, and the cheese should be melted.

Harissa Avocado Sausage and Egg Breakfast Panini

This Panini is filled with Mediterranean flavor. The Harissa and pepper jack give this some heat, the arugula provides a peppery flavor, and the Merguez has a beautiful spiced flavor.

Position: Closed　　　　　　　*Prep Time:* 15 Minutes
Selector: Grill/Panini　　　　　*Cook Time:* 6 Minutes
Plate Side: Grill or Griddle　　*Servings:* 2

Ingredients:

4 pieces of sourdough or crusty bread
¼ cup Harissa
2 eggs
½ avocado, sliced into pieces

1 cup pepper jack cheese
A handful of arugula
2 Merguez sausages, cooked
Olive oil
2 tsp butter

Directions:

> Use a whisk to beat the egg with a pinch of salt and pepper. Place the butter in a skillet and melt it on medium heat. Use a spoon to stir the eggs and push them across the pan. Cook until the eggs set, about 1 to 2 minutes.

> Chop the sausage into small pieces or butterfly them. Spread the Harissa on what's going to be the inside of two pieces of bread. Put a layer of egg on the Harissa side of the 2 pieces of bread, then the sausage, then the arugula, then avocado and top with the cheese. Then place the other two pieces of bread on top of the cheese. Brush the top and bottom of the sandwiches with olive oil.

> Preheat the Cuisinart Griddler to Medium-High with unit closed.

> Cook the Panini for 4 to 6 minutes, checking halfway through. The bread should be toasted, and the cheese should be melted.

Pancetta Cherry Tomato and Egg English Muffin Panini

This Panini features a variety of flavors. Pancetta is like an Italian form of bacon, the cherry tomatoes give it sweetness, and the mozzarella gives it creaminess.

Position: Closed
Selector: Grill/Panini
Plate Side: Grill or Griddle

Prep Time: 15 Minutes
Cook Time: 6 Minutes
Servings: 1

Ingredients:

1 English muffin
1 egg
5 cherry tomatoes
Fresh basil, chopped

2 slices of mozzarella
Olive oil
1 tsp butter
4 thin slices of pancetta, cooked

Directions:

> Use a whisk to beat the egg with a pinch of salt and pepper. Place the butter in a skillet and melt it on medium heat. Use a spoon to stir the eggs and push them across the pan. Cook until the eggs set, about 1 to 2 minutes.

> Put a layer of avocado on the Harissa side of the 2 pieces of bread, then the sausage, then the arugula, and top with the cheese. Then place the other two pieces of bread on top of the cheese. Brush the top and bottom of the sandwiches with olive oil.

> Preheat the Cuisinart Griddler to Medium-High with unit closed.

> Cook the Panini 4 to 6 minutes, checking halfway through. The bread should be toasted, and the cheese should be melted.

Goat Cheese Pesto and Egg English Muffin Panini

This Panini features some lovely contrasting flavors. The goat cheese has a strong flavor that's tempered by the aromatic flavor of the peso, and the rich flavor of the eggs. If you're not a fan of goat cheese try using half as much goat cheese or no goat cheese at all! It's truly a treat anyway you decide to make it!

Position: Closed
Selector: Grill/Panini
Plate Side: Grill or Griddle

Prep Time: 20 Minutes
Cook Time: 5 Minutes
Servings: 4

Ingredients:

4 eggs
4 English muffins, split and lightly toasted
4 tbsps. prepared pesto
4 oz. Humboldt Fog goat cheese or Bucheron de chevre, sliced into 4 rounds

4 large tomato slices
8 leaves radicchio
Olive oil
4 tsp butter

Directions:

❯ Use a whisk to beat the eggs with a pinch of salt and pepper. Place the butter in a skillet and melt it on medium heat. Use a spoon to stir the eggs and push them across the pan. Cook until the eggs set, about 1 to 2 minutes.

❯ Spread the pesto on the inside of part of the English muffins, then layer the eggs on the inside of the lower piece of the English muffin, then the cheese, then the radicchio, then the tomatoes, and top with the other half of the English muffin. Brush the top and bottom of the sandwiches with olive oil.

❯ Preheat the Cuisinart Griddler to Medium-High with unit closed.

❯ Cook the Panini for 4 to 5 minutes, checking halfway through. The English muffin should be toasted, and the cheese should be melted.

Bruschetta

Culinary Caprese Bruschetta

This part-perfect appetizer will have your friends asking for this wonderful recipe that will be the hit at any party for friends or family.

Position: Closed
Selector: Grill/Panini
Plate Side: Grill or Griddle

Prep Time: 20 Minutes
Cook Time: 5 Minutes
Servings: 6-8

Ingredients:

8 ounces of balsamic vinegar
8 ounces of fresh Mozzarella
2 tbsp. fresh chopped basil

2 cups cherry tomatoes
1 French baguette loaf

Directions:

> Heat the balsamic vinegar into a small pan or skillet.
> You will heat this oil at low/medium temperature. You will know when it is ready when it slowly comes to a light boil.
> Let it simmer…about 6-8 minutes. Then the vinegar will start thickening while it is cooking. As it is cooking the amount in the pan will shrink to about half, when it does this, cut off the heat.
> Pour all of the vinegar into a container to cool off. It will thicken the more it cools and will be more like a glaze.
> Take the mozzarella and chop it up.
> Cut the tomatoes in thirds.
> Chop the basil into strips and mix the tomatoes, mozzarella and basil.
> Slice the baguette into desired slice size. 1-2" thick. If you want to toast, then put the slices down on the panini press and cover with butter or olive oil.
> Preheat the Cuisinart Griddler to Medium-High with unit closed.
> Cook for 1-2 minutes until golden brown.
> Serve with the bruschetta on top of the baguette and a balsamic glaze drizzle on top.

Early Morning Breakfast Bruschetta

There's nothing like waking up to the taste of a great breakfast bruschetta. A great way to start the day off right! This one is yummy!

Position: Closed
Selector: Grill/Panini
Plate Side: Grill or Griddle

Prep Time: 20 Minutes
Cook Time: 5 Minutes
Servings: 4-5

Ingredients:

French bread (sliced 1" thick)
3 Tbsp. unsalted butter, divided
4 large eggs
1/4 cup whole milk

1 Tbsp. chopped chives
1/8 tsp. fresh black pepper
3/4 cup mashed avocado
1 cup diced tomatoes

Directions:

> Brush 2 tablespoons of the melted butter.
> Brush both sides of each slice. Preheat the Cuisinart Griddler to Medium-High with unit closed.
> Place the bread slices on griddler for 2 about minutes until toasted and set it aside.
> Whisk together the eggs, chives, milk and pepper in a medium bowl.
> Get a medium nonstick pan over medium-low heat and add the rest of the butter (1 tablespoon) in the pan.
> Pour the eggs in and scramble to your liking.
> Spread a small part of the mashed avocado on one side of each piece of the toast. Last...put the avocado with the scrambled eggs on top and garnish with the diced tomatoes.

Balsamic Vinegar & Garlic Bruschetta

This part-perfect appetizer will have your friends asking for this wonderful recipe that will be the hit at any party for friends or family.

Position: Closed
Selector: Grill/Panini
Plate Side: Grill or Griddle

Prep Time: 20 Minutes
Cook Time: 5 Minutes
Servings: 6-8

Ingredients:

8 diced tomatoes
1/3 cup chopped fresh basil
1/4 cup shredded Parmesan cheese
2 cloves garlic, minced
1 tbsp. balsamic vinegar

1 tsp. olive oil
1/4 tsp. kosher salt
1/4 tsp. freshly ground black pepper
1 loaf French bread, toasted and sliced

Directions:

> Toss together in a bowl or container the tomatoes, basil, Parmesan cheese, and garlic.
> Combine the balsamic vinegar, olive oil, kosher salt, and pepper. Preheat the Cuisinart Griddler on Medium-High with unit closed.
> Place the bread slices on griddler for 2 about minutes until toasted and set it aside.
> You will now serve the toast and take the mixture to be spread on the toasted bread.
> Enjoy

Fresh Garlic Tomato Bruschetta

Nothing beats the taste of fresh tomato and garlic as a combination and powerful punch on the taste buds. This is one of those "Grab em' before they're gone" kind of dish!

Position: Closed
Selector: Grill/Panini
Plate Side: Grill or Griddle

Prep Time: 20 Minutes
Cook Time: 5 Minutes
Servings: 4-6

Ingredients

1/2 pound ripe tomatoes, at room temperature (3 to 4 medium)
Salt and fresh ground black pepper, to taste
2 tbsp. extra virgin olive oil
6 basil leaves, thinly sliced
Six 1/2" thick slices Italian or French bread
2 cloves garlic, peeled and left whole

Directions

> Take tomatoes and half them, removing and discarding most of the seeds.

> Cut tomatoes into medium chunks, then adding them to a medium bowl. Add salt, black pepper, to taste, basil and one tablespoon of olive oil. Stir and let sit several minutes to marinade the flavors together.

> Spread the rest of the oil on the bread slices. Preheat Cuisinart Griddler to Medium-High with unit closed.

> Place the bread slices on griddler for 2 about minutes until toasted and set it aside.

> Spread garlic on one side of the bread while it is still warm.

> Stir the tomato mix again to see if it needs added seasoning. Spoon a nice helping on each slice. Spread some of the juice that is left at the bottom of the bowl on top of the tomatoes.

Spicy Bruschetta with Dijon

You would never think of putting a little Dijon on a piece of toasted bread to make a Bruschetta till now. This is freaking amazing and you have to try it to believe it. So here it is for you!

Position: Closed
Selector: Grill/Panini
Plate Side: Grill or Griddle

Prep Time: 20 Minutes
Cook Time: 5 Minutes
Servings: 4-6

Ingredients
1 baguette, cut in half long ways
2 tsp. minced garlic (jar is fine)
3 tbsp. extra-virgin olive oil
1/4 cup grated parmesan cheese
2 1/2 cups minced tomatoes (cut really fine till pasty)
1 tbsp. Dijon mustard
1/3 cup thinly sliced fresh basil leaf
2 tbsp. balsamic vinegar
1/2 tsp. salt
1 tsp. fresh ground pepper

Directions
> Add the tomatoes, garlic, basil, vinegar, olive oil, cheese, salt and pepper in a bowl or container.
> Mix up very good and let sit for at least 20 minutes at room temperature.
> The flavors will marinade over this time to blend together. Preheat the Cuisinart Griddler to Medium-High with unit closed.
> Slice the bread into individual pieces and place the bread slices on griddler for 2 about minutes until toasted.
> Spoon the mixture on top of the toasted bread and enjoy.

The Ultimate Bacon Bruschetta

Did I hear someone just say??? If you guessed bacon... then you are correct! Bacon goes well on literally anything and these delightful and tasty treats may have you making this one for an entire week!

Position: Closed
Selector: Grill/Panini
Plate Side: Grill or Griddle

Prep Time: 20 Minutes
Cook Time: 5 Minutes
Servings: 4-6

Ingredients

6 bacon strips, chopped
4 ciabatta rolls
2 tbsp. olive oil
2 medium tomatoes, seeded and chopped
1/4 tsp. salt
1/8 tsp. pepper
3/4 cup crumbled feta cheese
16 fresh basil leaves, thinly sliced
1/2 cup balsamic vinaigrette

Directions

> Cook bacon over medium heat until crisp in a pan or skillet. You can also cook the bacon in your Cuisinart Griddler if desired.
> Drain the bacon on a paper towel of some sort.
> Cut rolls in half, then cut each half into quarters.
> Brush both sides of the bread with oil. Preheat the Cuisinart Griddler to Medium-High with unit closed.
> Place the bread slices on griddler for 5 about minutes until toasted.
> Mix the tomatoes, salt and pepper in a bowl of some kind.
> Put on top of each piece of toasted bread the tomato mixture, cheese, basil bacon and drizzle with vinaigrette.
> Serve immediately while toast is still warm.

Delicious Chocolate Bacon Bruschetta

We mentioned that bacon goes good on almost anything and this is one of those dishes you just have to try for yourself. A taste but twister for sure!!

Position: Closed
Selector: Grill/Panini
Plate Side: Grill or Griddle

Prep Time: 20 Minutes
Cook Time: 2 Minutes
Servings: 4-6

Ingredients

4 slices bacon
9 thin slices of sourdough
baguette

olive oil, or as needed
3 ounces miniature chocolate
chips

Directions

> Cook bacon over medium heat until crisp in a pan or skillet. You can also cook the bacon in your Cuisinart Griddler if desired.
> Drain the bacon on a paper towel of some sort. When it cools, crumble the bacon.
> Brush both sides of the bread with oil.
> Mix crumbled bacon with chocolate chips in a bowl and top each baguette slice with a small amount of the mixture. Preheat the Gridder to Medium-High with unit closed.
> Place the bread slices on griddler and pull down till the top is about 1" from the chocolate bread slices. Heat for about 2 minutes until the chocolate chips are soft but still firm.
> Enjoy!

Parmesan Cheese-n-Peas Bruschetta

Like mom used to tell you..." Eat your peas!!!" So, we brought this dish to you from an inspired chef who used to have this said to them frequently when they were younger. You will love this dish as much as we did! Enjoy!

Position: Closed
Selector: Grill/Panini
Plate Side: Grill or Griddle

Prep Time: 20 Minutes
Cook Time: 2 Minutes
Servings: 4-5

Ingredients

12 slices of baguette bread
1/2 garlic clove
1 cup peas (thawed fresh or froze),
Kosher salt

2 tbsp.-virgin olive oil
Shaved Parmesan
Torn mint
A few drops of balsamic vinegar

Directions

> Preheat the Cuisinart Griddler to Medium-High with unit closed. Place the bread slices on griddler for 2 about minutes until toasted.
> Then rub the toast with the garlic clove to coat.
> Blanch peas in a medium pan of boiling salted water till they turn a little tender.
> Drain the peas and move them to a bowl and sprinkle with sea salt and virgin olive oil. Mash the peas with back of a fork.
> Use a tablespoon and spread mixture on the toasted bread. Top with Parmesan cheese, mint, and just a hint of balsamic vinegar.

Big Flavorful Burgers

The "BIG" El Niño

This burger isn't for the weak of heart. It adds a little punch and crunch to your palate; making you going back for more. Keep this recipe close because it's gonna be a hit at the table.

Position: Closed
Selector: Grill/Panini
Plate Side: Grill or Griddle

Prep Time: 20 Minutes
Cook Time: 10 Minutes
Servings: 3

Ingredients:

1 pound ground buffalo
2 tsp. taco seasoning
1/3 cup salsa
¼ cup guacamole
¼ cup sour cream
3 diced habaneros

Lettuce, shredded
1 diced tomato
3 slices of Pepper Jack Cheese
12-14 French fried onion rings.
Any will do.
3 hamburger buns

Directions:

> Mix the sour cream and guacamole together in a separate bowl and set to the side.

> Dice the ham. Mix the ham and taco seasoning in with the ground buffalo until well mixed.

> Form the ground buffalo mixture into 6 equal sized balls. Turn each ball into a patty by pressing it in your hands into a patty.

> Preheat the Cuisinart Griddler to Sear with unit closed.

> Put the patties on the griddler and cook for 3 minutes. Check the burgers to make sure they are to your doneness, depending on thickness!

> Next, open up the griddler and place the cheese on each burger, and grill for an additional 2 minutes until cheese is melted.

> Put as many of the onion rings on the griddler and cook for about 3-5 min. if frozen. About 2-3 min if thawed. Check till done.

> Serve on a bun with habaneros, diced tomatoes, shredded lettuce, French fried onion rings.

The Beefed-Up Burger

Doubling up the patties gives you all the beef you can handle. Mixing it with the classic burger condiments will bring you back to your childhood.

Position: Closed
Selector: Grill/Panini
Plate Side: Grill or Griddle

Prep Time: 20 Minutes
Cook Time: 5 Minutes
Servings: 1

Ingredients:

1 tbsp. finely chopped onion
1 tbsp. ketchup
1 tsp. prepared mustard
1/4 tsp. salt
1/8 tsp. pepper
1 pound lean ground beef
(90% lean)

1/4 cup finely shredded cheddar cheese
1 hamburger bun split
Lettuce leaves and tomato slices, optional

Directions:

> Combine the onion, ketchup, mustard, cheese, salt and pepper in a bowl. Mix these ingredients with the beef.
> Form the ground beef mixture into four 8 oz. balls. Turn each ball into a burger patty by pressing it in your hands.
> Preheat the Cuisinart Griddler to Sear with unit closed. Place onions on the griddler and cook for 2 minutes with olive oil and the rest of the salt and pepper.
> Put the patties on the griddler and cook for 3 minutes on each side. Check for you desired doneness.
> Serve: on a bun with lettuce and tomato if desired. (optional)

The Artery Clogger

This is the monster burger of all burgers. Layered with two grilled cheese sandwiches and topped with onion rings, this burger will be a towering, mess of cheesy goodness.

Position: Closed
Selector: Grill/Panini
Plate Side: Grill or Griddle

Prep Time: 20 Minutes
Cook Time: 3 Minutes
Servings: 4

Ingredients:
1 pound ground beef
1 cup mushrooms, sliced
8 frozen onion rings, thawed
12 slices of cheddar cheese

4 slices of Swiss cheese
16 slices of Texas Toast
Iceberg lettuce
Secret Sauce

Secret Sauce:
½ cup Ketchup
½ cup mayonnaise
1 dill pickle, diced

Directions:
> Prepare onion rings to package directions.
> Preheat the Cuisinart Griddler to Sear with unit closed.
> Fry bacon in the griddler until it is done to your liking.
> Prepare 8 grilled cheese sandwiches with one set of cheddar cheese in each.
> Combine all secret sauce ingredients.
> Sauté mushrooms in butter until brown.
> Form the burger mixture into four 8 ounce balls. Turn each ball into a patty by using your hands to press into a burger patty.
> Grill burgers for 3 minutes.
> Serve: grilled cheese sandwich, burger patty, one slice of cheddar and Swiss cheese, 2 slices of bacon, sautéed mushrooms, 2 onions rings, secret sauce, lettuce and top with remaining grilled cheese sandwich...WOW!!! What an Amazing Burger!

147

Nothing but The Beef

The sourdough really lets the taste of the beef shine through. Cheddar in the middle complements the taste of the meat.

Position: Closed
Selector: Grill/Panini
Plate Side: Grill or Griddle

Prep Time: 20 Minutes
Cook Time: 12 Minutes
Servings: 4

Ingredients:

1 ½ pounds lean ground beef
¾ tsp. plus 1/8 tsp. salt
¼ tsp. plus 1/8 tsp. black pepper
2 oz. shredded cheddar cheese
4 red onion slices

2 tbsp. extra virgin olive oil
4 crusty sourdough bread slices
4 tsp. course-grained Dijon mustard
12 plum tomato slices

Directions:

> Combine the ground beef, cheese and ¾ tsp. salt and ¼ tsp. pepper into a bowl.
> Form the ground beef mixture into four 8 oz. balls. Turn each ball into a burger patty by pressing it in your hands.
> Place onions in a pan and cook for 4 minutes with olive oil and the rest of the salt and pepper.
> Preheat the Cuisinart Griddler to Sear with unit closed. Put the patties on the griddler and cook for 6 minutes on each side.
> Serve on a bun and top with spread the Dijon mustard. Top with an onion and tomato on top of the burger patty.

Mustard glazed "knock out" burger

The Mustard Glazed Burger pairs the spiciness of the grain mustard and compliments it with the dill pickle, flavors that will have you asking why you never glazed your burgers before.

Position: Closed
Selector: Grill/Panini
Plate Side: Grill or Griddle

Prep Time: 20 Minutes
Cook Time: 3 Minutes
Servings: 4

Ingredients:

1½ lbs. lean ground beef
Kosher Salt
Fresh Ground Pepper
½ cup grain Mustard

1 tsp. garlic powder
4 slices of Pepper Jack Cheese
16 dill pickle chips (diced)

Directions:

> Mix the ground buffalo, salt, pepper, ¼ Dijon Mustard sauce, shredded cheese, dill pickle and garlic powder into a bowl.
> Form the ground beef mixture into four 8 oz. balls. Turn each ball into a burger patty by pressing it in your hands.
> Brush the patties with grain mustard on both sides
> Preheat the Cuisinart Griddler to Sear with unit closed. Put the patties on the griddler and cook for 3 minutes. Put some more of the mustard on the patties before they are done cooking to glaze them.
> Serve: Put the remaining grain mustard on a roll and top with lettuce and tomato.

Completely "Comatosed"

This is the burger to top all burgers. What better than a sweet creamy donut as a bun. The sweetness of the bun is the perfect addition to brunch with the ladies, especially when you want to provide more than just coffee and donuts.

Position: Closed
Selector: Grill/Panini
Plate Side: Grill or Griddle

Prep Time: 20 Minutes
Cook Time: 6 Minutes
Servings: 3

Ingredients:

¾ pound ground beef
3 tbsp. parsley, chopped
2 tbsp. onion, grated
House seasoning
2 tbsp. butter
3 eggs
6 slices bacon, cooked
6 glazed donuts

House seasoning:

1 cup salt
¼ cup black pepper
¼ cup garlic powder

Directions:

> Combine the meat, parsley and onion together.
> Form the ground beef mixture into four 8 oz. balls. Turn each ball into a burger patty by pressing it in your hands.
> Preheat the Cuisinart Griddler to Sear with unit closed. Cook burgers on griddler for 3 minutes on each side.
> Fry bacon in the panini press until cooked to your liking.
> Cook eggs in a pan or on the grill, adding butter so they do not stick. Be careful when taking it out. Cook until the yolks are nice and set.
> Place patties on donuts; top each with 2 pieces of bacon and an egg and serve with coffee or juice.

For the Love of Bison

The Tarragon pairs perfectly with the bison and allows it shine. We keep the ingredients to a minimum, so the bison takes center stage.

Position: Closed
Selector: Grill/Panini
Plate Side: Grill or Griddle

Prep Time: 20 Minutes
Cook Time: 3 Minutes
Servings: 4

INGREDIENTS:

2 pounds lean ground bison
1 tsp. dried tarragon
1/4 cup chopped parsley
1 ½ cups of diced onions

2/3 cups mushrooms
salt and pepper to taste
3/4 cup blue cheese, crumbled
2 tomatoes (sliced into rings)

DIRECTIONS:

❯ Place the onions and mushrooms in a pan and cook for 5 minutes. Add the parsley and set to the side to cool.
❯ Combine the bison, blue cheese, parsley, mushrooms and tarragon in a bowl.
❯ Form the ground beef mixture into four 8 oz. balls. Turn each ball into a burger patty by pressing it in your hands.
❯ Preheat the Cuisinart Griddler to Sear with unit closed. Put the patties on the griddler and cook for 3 minutes.
❯ Serve with cheese and tomato slices.

The "Maniac" Burger

If you are a tomato lover then this is the burger for you. This fresh herb piece of meat will bring your summer to life.

Position: Closed
Selector: Grill/Panini
Plate Side: Grill or Griddle

Prep Time: 20 Minutes
Cook Time: 3 Minutes
Servings: 6

Ingredients:

3 pounds ground chuck
5 tbsp. sun-dried tomato paste
Kosher Salt
4 ounces crumbled goat cheese
3 minced garlic cloves
3 tbsp. torn fresh basil
2 tsp. garlic salt

12 whole sun-dried tomatoes
packed in oil, chopped in half
6 slices of goat cheese
6 Kaiser Rolls
½ cup mayonnaise
24 large fresh basil leaves

Directions:

> Mix first seven ingredients into a bowl.
> Form the ground beef mixture into four 8 oz. balls. Turn each ball into a burger patty by pressing it in your hands.
> Preheat the Cuisinart Griddler to Sear with unit closed. Put the patties on the griddler. Press down and cook for 3 minutes.
> Spread mayonnaise on a roll and garnish with 2 basil leaves on the top and bottom of the burger. Add cheese then the bun.

The Oh So Green Machine

This recipe is packed with a ton of flavor and on a warm summer day you can choose to ditch the bun and eat on top of a bed of lettuce instead. It's your choice. Why not make it a good one?

Position: Closed
Selector: Grill/Panini
Plate Side: Grill or Griddle

Prep Time: 20 Minutes
Cook Time: 3 Minutes
Servings: 6

Ingredients:

Burger:

3 lbs. lean ground turkey
3 green onions, finely chopped
2 cloves garlic, minced
2 tbsp. fresh parsley, finely chopped
1 tbsp. fresh sage, finely chopped

2 tbsp. Dijon mustard
2 large eggs
¼ cup almond flour
1 tsp. salt
½ tsp. ground white pepper
1 ½ ripe avocado, sliced

Spicy Mayo:

¼ cup paleo mayo
¼ tsp. garlic powder
Pinch salt
½ chipotle powder

Leftover avocado slices from burgers
Arugula
Romaine
Kale

Directions:

> Burgers: Combine all burger ingredients, but not avocado, kale, arugula, and romaine into a bowl.
> Cut the avocados in half and slice into three slices. Toss the remaining parts of the avocado into another bowl.
> Form the ground turkey mixture into four 8 oz. balls. Turn each ball into a burger patty by pressing it in your hands.
> Preheat the Cuisinart Griddler to Sear with unit closed. Put the patties on the griddler. Press down and cook for 3 minutes.
> Put the patties on the grill and cook for 3 minutes.
> Serve on a bun and top with mayo, avocado, kale, arugula, and romaine.

Veggiemania

This recipe showcases squash and elevates it from a lowly side dish to a main dish. Here squash is the star of the show and once you try it, you will understand why.

Position: Closed
Selector: Grill/Panini
Plate Side: Grill or Griddle

Prep Time: 20 Minutes
Cook Time: 3 Minutes
Servings: 4

Ingredients:

1 delicata squash, halved
lengthwise and seeded
2 tbsp. olive oil (optional)
 salt and ground black pepper to
taste
 2 tbsp. butter
1 shallot, minced
1 clove garlic, minced

6 sun-dried tomatoes, chopped
1 cup bread crumbs, or more if
needed
1 egg, beaten
1/4 cup grated Parmesan cheese
1/4 cup vegetable oil, or as
needed

Directions:

> Put squash on a baking sheet, sprinkle with olive oil and cook for 40 minutes at 470 degrees. Cut into cubes when it cools down.
> Cook and stir shallots and garlic in butter for 10 minutes. Stir in sun-dried tomatoes and avocado. Cook for 3 more minutes.
> Combine all Spicy Mayo ingredients in a bowl. Smash with a fork.
> Add the squash to this mixture, mash and let cool down.
> Combine bread crumbs, the egg and parmesan cheese into the squash mixture.
> Form the ground squash mixture into four 8 oz. balls. Turn each ball into a burger patty by pressing it in your hands.
> Put the last 1 tablespoon of olive oil on the grill so it browns and does not stick. Make sure you brush some on the top grill plates.
> Preheat the Cuisinart Griddler to Sear with unit closed. Put the patties on the griddler. Press down and cook for 3 minutes or till brown and ready.
> Serve on a whole wheat bun and choose the condiments that would work best for this burger.

Yummy Griddler Pizza's

Succulent Basil Pesto Pizza

Well Pizza is Back! We've got you covered in this department so no need to worry. Quick, easy, fun and deliciously wonderful for you, friends and family! They'll love you for it.

Position: Flat
Selector: Griddle
Plate Side: Griddle

Prep Time: 20 Minutes
Cook Time: 8 Minutes
Servings: 6

Ingredients:
2 tbsp. cooking spray (or olive oil)
1 pound fresh pizza dough
1/3 cup basil pesto

12 oz. fresh mozzarella (shredded)
> 2 oz. shaved ham

Directions:
> Divide the pizza dough into 6 sections.
> Preheat the Cuisinart Griddler to 425 with unit closed. Open unit to extend flat.
> Brush or spray the oil on the griddler.
> Stretch 1 piece of dough into a round shape. May have to repeat for the dough has elastic features.
> Spread two to three tablespoons of pesto on the stretched dough.
> Sprinkle the ham, then top with cheese.
> Place the dough on the griddle and closed the lid leaving it 1 inch from the top of the pizza.
> Grill the pizza until the dough is cooked, cheese is melted/bubbly and lightly brown. About 6 to 8 minutes. Slice and serve.

Mouthwatering Marinara Pepperoni Pizza

A traditional dish that you can't get off of your mind. The marinara sauce brings out the flavors of the vegetables nicely in this particular dish. Yes, a classic, but yet delicious. Enjoy!

Position: Flat
Selector: Griddle
Plate Side: Griddle

Prep Time: 20 Minutes
Cook Time: 8 Minutes
Servings: 6

Ingredients:

2 tbsp. cooking spray
(or virgin olive oil)
1 pound fresh pizza dough
1/3 cup marinara sauce
12 oz. fresh mozzarella
(shredded)

2 oz. pepperoni
½ stick butter (grass fed)
1 tbsp. diced green onions
1 tsp. garlic powder

Directions:

> Divide the pizza dough into 6 sections.
> Preheat the Cuisinart Griddler to 425 with unit closed. Open unit to extend flat.
> Brush or spray the oil on the griddler.
> Stretch 1 piece of dough into a round shape. May have to repeat for the dough has elastic features.
> Spread two to three tablespoons of the marinara sauce on the stretched dough covering evenly.
> Add the pepperoni, garlic, tomatoes, olives then top with cheese.
> Place the dough on the griddle and closed the lid leaving it 1 inch from the top of the pizza.
> Grill the pizza until the dough is cooked, cheese is melted/bubbly and lightly brown. About 6 to 8 minutes. Set aside to cool.
> Melt butter in a small pan.
> Add garlic and onions. Simmer 2-3 minutes. (for dipping crust)
> Slice and serve.

Mediterranean Greek Pesto Pizza

We are bringing this one to you all the way from Greece. This wonderful delight is something you would make on a nice movie night. Crispy crust, simple and quick and great to eat.

Position: Flat
Selector: Griddle
Plate Side: Griddle

Prep Time: 20 Minutes
Cook Time: 8 Minutes
Servings: 6

Ingredients:

2 tbsp. cooking spray (or olive oil)
1 pound fresh pizza dough
1/3 cup marinara sauce
1 tbsp. garlic powder
1/2 tomato (sliced)

12 oz. fresh mozzarella (shredded)
¼ cup black olives (sliced)
¼ cup feta cheese
3 pepperoncini's
2 oz. shaved ham
Tzatziki sauce (to dip)

Directions:

❭ Divide the pizza dough into 6 sections.
❭ Preheat the Cuisinart Griddler to 425 with unit closed. Open the unit to extend flat.
❭ Brush or spray the oil on the griddler.
❭ Stretch 1 piece of dough into a round shape. May have to repeat for the dough has elastic features.
❭ Spread two to three tablespoons of marinara sauce on the stretched dough.
❭ Sprinkle the garlic powder, tomatoes, ham, black olives, feta cheese, pepperoncini's and last top with cheese.
❭ Place the dough on the griddle and closed the lid leaving it 1 inch from the top of the pizza.
❭ Grill the pizza until the dough is cooked, cheese is melted/bubbly and lightly brown. About 6 to 8 minutes.
❭ Slice and serve. Make sure you're use the Tzatziki sauce (to dip)

Italian Pepperoni Lovers Pizza

We are bringing this one to you all the way from Greece. This wonderful delight is something you would make on a nice movie night. Crispy crust, simple and quick and great to eat.

Position: Flat
Selector: Griddle
Plate Side: Griddle

Prep Time: 20 Minutes
Cook Time: 8 Minutes
Servings: 6

Ingredients:

2 tbsp. cooking spray (or olive oil)
1 pound fresh pizza dough
1/3 cup basil pesto
1 tbsp. garlic powder

12 oz. fresh mozzarella (shredded)
25 slices of pepperoni
Italian dressing (to dip)

Directions:

> Divide the pizza dough into 6 sections.
> Preheat the Cuisinart Griddler to 425 with unit closed. Open the unit to extend flat.
> Brush or spray the oil on the griddler.
> Stretch 1 piece of dough into a round shape. May have to repeat for the dough has elastic features.
> Spread two to three tablespoons of pesto on the stretched dough.
> Layer the pepperoni, add cheese then add more pepperoni on top.
> Place the dough on the griddle and closed the lid leaving it 1 inch from the top of the pizza.
> Grill the pizza until the dough is cooked, cheese is melted/bubbly and lightly brown. About 6 to 8 minutes. Italian dressing to dip!

It's the Weekend Pizza

Sometimes, some of the best things are made simple. This is a pizza you can eat any day of the week, but the flavors of this one will get you going on any weekend occasion.

Position: Flat
Selector: Griddle
Plate Side: Griddle

Prep Time: 20 Minutes
Cook Time: 8 Minutes
Servings: 6

Ingredients:

2 tbsp. cooking spray (or olive oil)
1 pound fresh pizza dough
1/3 cup basil pesto
1 tbsp. garlic powder

12 oz. fresh mozzarella (shredded)
12 - 15 slices of pepperoni
¼ cup black olives (sliced)
¼ cup red onions (sliced)

Directions:

> Divide the pizza dough into 6 sections.
> Preheat the Cuisinart Griddler to 425 with unit closed. Open unit to extend flat.
> Brush or spray the oil on the griddler.
> Stretch 1 piece of dough into a round shape. May have to repeat for the dough has elastic features.
> Spread two to three tablespoons of pesto on the stretched dough.
> Layer the pizza evenly with the pepperoni, onion and olive slices. Then shower the cheese on top.
> Place the dough on the griddle and closed the lid leaving it 1 inch from the top of the pizza.
> Grill the pizza until the dough is cooked, cheese is melted/bubbly and lightly brown. About 6 to 8 minutes.

Peanut and Jelly Pizza

The kiddo's just love this one! Let the kids help you with this delightful dish. It is one that will keep them smiling for a little while and yummy for their tummy!

Position: Flat
Selector: Griddle
Plate Side: Griddle

Prep Time: 20 Minutes
Cook Time: 3 Minutes
Servings: 6

Ingredients:

2 tbsp. cooking spray (or olive oil)
1 pound fresh pizza dough

1/3 cup peanut butter
1/3 cup of jam (any flavor)
½ tsp. cinnamon

Directions:

> Divide the pizza dough into 6 sections.
> Preheat the Cuisinart Griddler to 425 with unit closed. Open unit to extend flat.
> Brush or spray the oil on the griddler.
> Stretch 1 piece of dough into a round shape. May have to repeat for the dough has elastic features.
> Spread the peanut butter, then jelly on the stretched dough.
> Sprinkle the cinnamon on top lightly.
> Place the dough on the griddle and closed the lid leaving it 1 inch from the top of the pizza.
> Grill the pizza until the dough is cooked, bubbly and lightly brown. The crust may bubble. About 2 to 3 minutes. Let it cool, slice and serve.

Next Up on the List!

Show Us Some Love... ☺

PLEASE LEAVE US A REVIEW!

Leave us a review on Amazon where you purchased this book!

>>> Amazon.com/dp/1729785018 <<<

In the world of an author who writes books independently, your reviews are not only touching but important so that we know you like the material we have prepared for "you" our audience! So, leave us a review...we would love to see your honest feedback!

Hello all...I am very excited that you have purchased one of my publications. I've poured my heart into these warm recipes that I have prepared for you in this book. Hope you enjoy, with a warm heart!

~Elana Cordova
"Personal & Professional Chef"

Bonus Gift for You!

Get Em' Before You Can Buy Em'!

Get your very own personal copy of our newest cookbooks when they pre-launch! Giving you an experience to keep in your home to test out what our authors have put their hearts into!

GET YOURS NOW! Just click the button or go to the link below! ***Enjoy!***

HealthyLifestyleRecipes.org/FreeBook2Review

Metric Volume, metric weight and oven temperature charts are tools that everyone wants in the kitchen, but are never around when you need them. That's why we have created these charts for you so you never skip a beat when you're cooking! Hope this helps! :)

Metric Volume Conversions Chart

US Volume Measure		Metric Equivalent
1/8 tsp.		0.5 milliliters
1/4 tsp.		1 milliliter
1/2 tsp.		2.5 milliliters
3/4 tsp.		4 milliliters
1 tsp.		5 milliliters
1 1/4 tsps.		6 milliliters
1 1/2 tsps.		7.5 milliliters
1 3/4 tsps.		8.5 milliliters
2 tsps.		10 milliliters
1/2 tbsp.		7.5 milliliters
1 tbsp.	(3 tsps. 1/2 fluid ounce)	15 milliliters
2 tbsp.	(1 fluid ounce)	30 milliliters
1/4 cup	(4 tbsps.)	60 milliliters
1/3 cup		90 milliliters
1/2 cup	(4 fluid ounces)	125 milliliters
2/3 cup		160 milliliters
3/4 cup	(6 fluid ounces)	180 milliliters
1 cup	(16 tbsps., 8 fluid ounces)	250 milliliters
1 1/4 cups		300 milliliters
1 1/2 cups	(12 fluid ounces)	360 milliliters
1 2/3 cups		400 milliliters
2 cups	(1 pint)	500 Milliliters
3 cups		700 Milliliters
4 cups	(1 quart)	950 milliliters
1 quart plus 1/4 cup		1 liter
4 quarts	(1 gallon)	3.8 liters

Metric Weight Conversion Chart

US Weight Measure		Metric Equivalent
1/2 ounce		7 grams
1/2 ounce		15 grams
3/4 ounce		21 grams
1 ounce		28 grams
1 1/4 ounces		35 grams
1 1/2 ounces		42.5 grams
1 2/3 ounces		45 grams
2 ounces		57 grams
3 ounces		85 grams
4 ounces	(1/4 lb.)	113 grams
5 ounces		142 grams
6 ounces		170 grams
7 ounces		198 grams
8 ounces	(1/2 lb.)	227 grams
12 ounces	(3/4 lb.)	340 grams
16 ounces	(1 lb.)	454 grams
32.5 ounce	(2.2 lbs.)	1 kilogram

Temperature Conversion Chart (°F/°C)

Degrees Fahrenheit	Degrees Celsius	Cool to Hot
200° F	100° C	Very cool oven
250° F	120° C	Very cool oven
275° F	140° C	Cool oven
300° F	150° C	Cool oven
325° F	160° C	Very moderate oven
350° F	180° C	Moderate oven
375° F	190° C	Moderate oven
400° F	200° C	Moderately hot oven
425° F	220° C	Hot oven
450° F	230° C	Hot oven
475° F	246° C	Very hot oven

About the Author

Elana Cordova is a Skilled and Self Taught, Master of her Craft and Professional Gourmet Chef that has soared to a very high level in the cooking and dining industry. She has prepared quality meals in the home and Kitchens of Various Celebrities all over the united states. Though in high demand... She always finds time to create new recipes and share her cooking style and experience with all of you. She loves creating new tasty foods and recipes from her heart and soul, because she has a passion and love for cooking extraordinary and delicious foods to share with everyone!

"Thank you for your purchase of my book! Hoping it captures your and heart gives you many ideas to create some of what you can come up with from this Cast Iron Skillet book! Enjoy!" With a warm heart...

Elana Cordova, Professional Chef

Griddle Panini, Bruschetta & Pizza Recipes:

"Experiment with your own creations!". List all your new recipes. Surprise yourself with what you can create.

Recipe Name	Special Ingredients

Made in the USA
San Bernardino, CA
24 July 2020